THEODOR ADORNO AND FILM THEORY

THEODOR ADORNO AND FILM THEORY

THE FINGERPRINT OF SPIRIT

Brian Wall

First published in 2013 by PALGRAVE MACMILLAN® in the United States—a division of St. Martin's Press LLC, 175 Fifth Avenue, New York, NY 10010.

Where this book is distributed in the UK, Europe and the rest of the world, this is by Palgrave Macmillan, a division of Macmillan Publishers Limited, registered in England, company number 785998, of Houndmills, Basingstoke, Hampshire RG21 6XS.

Palgrave Macmillan is the global academic imprint of the above companies and has companies and representatives throughout the world.

Palgrave® and Macmillan® are registered trademarks in the United States, the United Kingdom, Europe and other countries.

ISBN-13: 978-1-137-30613-5

Library of Congress Cataloging-in-Publication Data

Wall, Brian, 1961-
    Theodor Adorno and film theory: the fingerprint of spirit / Brian Wall.
      pages cm
    ISBN 978-1-137-30613-5
    1. Motion pictures—Philosophy. 2. Adorno, Theodor W., 1903-1969—Aesthetics. I. Title.

    PN1995.W345 2013
    791.4301—dc23   2012039428

A catalogue record of the book is available from the British Library.

Design by Scribe Inc.

First edition: March 2013

10 9 8 7 6 5 4 3 2 1

Transferred to Digital Printing in 2013

For Wendy and Nadja

CONTENTS

FIGURES

Acknowledgments

I wish to gratefully acknowledge the assistance of former dean Don Nieman of Harpur College at Binghamton University for granting me a research leave to pursue this project. I benefited as well from a fellowship here at the Institute for Advanced Studies in the Humanities, for which I must thank the director, Bat-Ami Bar On, as well as the other fellows who offered generous feedback on some of this work. An early version of Chapter 4 appeared in *Camera Obscura* 69 (2008), and belated though it is, I wish to thank the editorial team there and Patricia White, Sharon Willis, and Sasha Torres in particular. My gratitude to Robyn Curtis and Desiree Browne of Palgrave—your patience was appreciated. And I must thank a number of friends and colleagues past and present who contributed their invaluable attention and rich insights at various points along the way: Michael Zryd, Tom McDonough, Todd McGowan, Tilottama Rajan, Matthew Rowlinson, Vincent Grenier, Ariana Gerstein, and Steven Shaviro. This poor litany can only be an insufficient response to their generosity.

THE FINGERPRINT
OF SPIRIT

> Every visit to the cinema leaves me, against all my vigilance, stupider and worse.
> —Theodor Adorno, *Minima Moralia*

Adorno at the movies—given his fearsome reputation as an implacable critic of film, such a venture must smack of futility, if not outright perversity. The well-known and widely anthologized "The Culture Industry: Enlightenment as Mass Deception" (Adorno and Horkheimer 2002, 94–136) stands as the beginning and, *mauvaise fois*, mostly the end of film studies's engagement with Adorno.

One powerful strategy to counter his reputation as an impenetrable elitist or mandarin aesthete is Miriam Hansen's: in a wealth of detailed and rigorous essays, culminating in the recent *Cinema and Experience* (2012), Hansen patiently weaves together the many cinematic references that abound in Adorno's texts, linking them always to his related thoughts on aesthetics, and also on history, sociology, and philosophy. Her ultimate aim is to discern amid these scattered points the lineaments of a cinematic aesthetics that Adorno never finally fleshed out. This entails a historicization of his engagement with film and technologically produced media, starting with his early writings on music, passing from *Dialectic of Enlightenment* and *Composing for the Films* (1947), through to late essays such as "The Culture Industry Reconsidered" (1963), and "Transparencies on Film" (1966) to culminate in his unfinished *Aesthetic Theory* (1970) itself. To counter all he excoriates as affirmative in film—from its industrial production to its ties to iconic representation to its instrumental ideologies—Hansen elaborates a rich countercurrent in his work, evoking affinities with writing and especially music that point toward evocative traces of another possible filmic practice that persists in his thought, though never programmatically given. She describes one of the forms it might take:

> From Adorno's late writings on music we can extrapolate a model of thinking about cinematic mobility that would complement phenomenological, vitalist, gestaltist, and neuropsychological approaches currently in discussion with an aesthetic perspective capable of historicizing and analyzing particular instances of film practice. We might imagine cinematic mobility as a striated dynamics governed by distinct and sometimes disparate temporalities—a multisensorial "moving carpet" (as Bloch wrote in 1914) made up of internally dynamic chunks, knots, or clusters of time and the relations among them, in tension with irreversible linear time and the forward movement of narrative or other principles of organization. (Hansen 247)

This is both a historical and a theoretical program that could only benefit film studies were it to be assayed, as it promises to link in a constellated form a broad range of aesthetic and philosophical modes. Hansen's is a necessarily historical work that keeps faith with Adorno's thought.

David Jennemann's immaculately researched and helpfully estranging *Adorno in America* (2007) adds another crucial piece to the puzzle, countering the cliché of Adorno's mandarin aloofness with a wealth of historical detail drawn from Adorno's years in New York and Los Angeles. What emerges is a portrait of a relentlessly public intellectual, everywhere and always engaged with film and radio—engaged finally with tracing the democratic and cultural possibilities that might emerge from a technological mass culture. As such the "Culture Industry" chapter and many other texts besides can never again be disparaged as the spiteful reaction of a snobbish émigré, having now had their rootedness in concrete and historical experience affirmed.

But here I will proceed in another direction. Despite the value of these and many other works that have attempted to introduce Adorno more fully into cultural thought—and there is a wealth of excellent introductions available[1]—their very sweep seems to stand in an odd relation to some aspects of Adorno's own thought. For one of the prevalent issues that arises from Adorno's aesthetics, philosophy, and sociology has everything to do with the fate of the particular. Indeed, the Culture Industry itself is reviled for its uniformity, for its assertion of a constraining identity. I wish to proceed then not from the point of view of these historical surveys of Adorno's work, valuable, even essential as they undoubtedly are, but rather from the inside out, beginning with the particular—such necessarily broad engagements need the dialectical complement of an engagement with particulars, here particular films. Less pressingly, perhaps, I feel the absence in Adorno's own work of a sustained analysis of a particular film.

This is necessary, too, to the extent that film studies now seeks to leave behind the putative excesses of "French" theory for a new "posttheoretical" age.[2] If film theory must now account for itself and leave behind its totalizing tendencies, it might do so by adopting another of Adorno's key methods: immanent critique. Ironically, both film theory and cultural studies approach specific films from a transcendent vantage point: theory often subsumes film into its preexisting system of thought, as does a more cultural analysis, the signal difference being that for the cultural historian of film those preexisting values are political and material rather than philosophical. Following Adorno I wish to proceed by immanent critique, seeking to remain within the terms of a particular film or text and fastening on the contradictions inherent there so that those contradictions might speak to the material conditions in which a film was made.

But such a consideration of the particular film also necessarily implies that particular films are meaningful, that they have a truth content, and that they are not necessarily reducible to the material contexts from which they emerge. Film has a cognitive content that persists alongside its aesthetic, affective, and ideological aspects and that is pointedly nonconceptual. Such a claim brings to a head the conflicting characterizations that inform theoretical and cultural analyses of film, with the former privileging an explicit or implicit valuation of film as art, while for the latter film is a commodity or ideology. Of course it is both—but in the context of film, and especially the narrative films I have chosen as my objects here, the latter is assumed while the former must always be proven. Adorno writes, "Technology opens up unlimited opportunities for art in the future, and even in the poorest motion pictures there are moments when such opportunities are strikingly apparent. But the same principle that has opened up these opportunities also ties them to big business" (Adorno and Eisler 2007, xxxvi), and while his own attention found more focus on an art that sought to renounce consumption, nonetheless there is here a crucial opportunity to ask if there persists in some filmic commodities a truth that resists commodification and exchange value.

What Adorno's thought gives a politically committed, materialist film studies is an unflinching and rigorous opportunity to scrutinize its unthought precepts, suggesting it must start not from a fixed agenda but from a utopian desire: a wish for freedom, for an end to suffering. It must do so not just to avoid dogmatism and contradiction—for Bordwell and Carroll (1996) the legacy of the heyday of theory—but also to recognize that film writes checks that cannot be cashed, continually promises freedom, happiness, and an amelioration of misery. The conclusion Adorno would have us draw from these unfulfilled promises is not simply that culture is sheer ideology but rather that there is not yet a social or political context in which such promises could be kept. I wish here to remain sensitive to and critical of the various broken promises of mass culture, but also continually to register the extent to which such promises always testify to their own impossibility in advance, in the unseasonable climate of late capitalism. The films I have selected offer opportunities to be considered in their own historical contexts, of course; but as well, each insists in a variety of ways on its own irreducibility to such contexts. Put slightly differently, much in these films goes without saying—and yet at the same time something within them never gets said but hangs there naggingly on the edge of awareness, as if these films—like art—cannot say what they are. As if they need theory.

My title comes from Adorno, whose lectures are beginning to be translated and published by Stanford. In rejecting such a preservation of his improvised lectures he says, "If I were to speak in the way that would be necessary to achieve the authority of a precise account I would be incomprehensible to my audience; nothing I say can do justice to what I demand from a text . . . The fact that everywhere today there is a tendency to record extempore speech and then to disseminate it is a symptom of the methods of the administered world which pins down the ephemeral word in order to hold the speaker to it. A tape recording is a kind of fingerprint of the living spirit" (Adorno 2001, 283). I will return to this resonant quotation in Chapter 2, but for now I would only like to mark the extent to which the dialectic is at work even here, even in a rejection of a technology of reproduction that, like film, seeks to fix identity. In an administered world technology—the tape recorder and for us film—nonetheless still attests to something liminal beyond it, yet real for all that: spirit.

CHAPTER 1

THE SUBJECT/
OBJECT OF CINEMA

THE MALTESE FALCON (1941)

Consider two roughly contemporary modernist works: Beckett's *Waiting for Godot*, which premiered in 1953, and Hitchcock's *Strangers on a Train* (1951). Both are, for what it's worth, canonical, and though they differ in their media, how they have been taken up into various economies of culture—the elite and the popular—and many more ways that would be exhausting to detail, what prompts my comparison and what even might be said to permit their alignment under the rubric of modernism has to do with their relation to the object, which then comes to inform their status as aesthetic objects themselves. *Godot*, as is well known, structures itself around a central absence that can never be redeemed or made good, and *Strangers* follows the adventures of a lighter. In the former the object's absence is felt by characters and audience alike as a bewildering loss that undoes the very possibility of meaning itself, and along with that the assumed integrity of character, the possibility of agency, and even the passage of time. In the latter the object's trajectory, its circulation and exchange, promotes a remarkably similar anxiety; and even if ultimately this object's presence is less traumatic than Godot's absence, its status as a McGuffin, as mere pretext, is belied by its elevation to a similarly structural role, in which it determines the network of relations among characters by virtue not just of its ambivalent presence or absence but of this uncanny elevation to a very nearly metaphysical principle. If we worry after the lighter—and such worry is essential to the success of the film itself, a marker of suspense—such unease springs in part from the promotion of a banal, mundane, and contingent commodity to the ultimate determining instance of what will come to be found to be meaningful or even pleasurable about the film as such.

The object is absent; the object is present. Yet one might be forgiven for wondering if in some sense Godot's absence is finally made good on the larger level of the play, as this absence comes to affirm the singularity—even the presence—of this modernist text itself, with this particularity, then, coming to stand for modernism's own aspirations to produce the absolutely unique and single thing that resists exchange. Then dialectically the troubling being of Hitchcock's lighter must also necessarily be marked by a kind of absence, as its own particularity—here, its nominal use value—is rigorously effaced consequential of its elevation into a well-nigh metaphysical principle; and even within the larger frame of Hitchcock's oeuvre its immanent and scandalous particularity and power wanes by virtue of its alignment with its analogues—the glass of milk in *Suspicion* (1941), the key in *Notorious* (1946), and so on—that are so often on offer. Through its repetition the McGuffin also affirms its status as a trope, and even sanctions, at the far end, this mode of cultural production itself, the repetitions and seriality that characterize so much narrative film from before Hitchcock to after.

This is not to uphold heroic modernism over and against the commodities of the Culture Industry but rather to suggest the extent to which they inherit the same problematic. For the problem is not that of the absent and the present but rather of the single and the multiple. We find a quintessentially modernist desire: that the work should be singular, particular; that it is *the* work and not a work among others; that the singular will trump the multiple, even enfold the multiple, as in Mallarmé's impossible dream of a "book of the world" or Joyce's similarly dreamy *Finnegans Wake*, single works that mean to include all others. We might even include Guy Debord's *Mémoires*, notoriously bound in industrial grade sandpaper so as to destroy the adjacent books on the shelf (or the mahogany coffee table beneath), here asserting its singularity via the negation of others; and *Godot* might fit in here, too, its central absence even more thoroughly negative than sandpaper. Yet even in this minimal list one might discern the impossibility of singularity itself and how it bespeaks its own necessary failure in advance—for there are many modernist monads. Conjoined with the modernist injunction to "make it new," with its implication of a history that the modernist monad is at once to register and from which it is to separate itself, singularity can only appear as contradiction. Here the aesthetic idealism of modernism shows its basis in the material world; and here modernism's aesthetic agenda evinces an affinity with the totalizing tendencies of philosophy and theory, under which swarms of particulars are compelled to submit to the concept, the idea. The one, singular, particular artwork seeks impossibly and variously to include, annihilate, transcend, or redeem all others, especially commodified mass culture, with which the modernist work is dialectically at one.[1]

For Frederic Jameson's Hegelian-Marxist aesthetics, such a logic speaks to modernism's desire for a transaesthetic vocation, the desire of art to be *more* than art, even transcend art, whether as praxis (Marx) or philosophy (Hegel)—but these perspectives imply a future, and a future in which art no longer seems necessary, whether because material exploitation and inequality have been resolved and no one needs a *promesse du bonheur* any longer (Marx) or because *geist* has shuffled off its material ballast (Hegel; these may be versions of the same unlikely event, if you ask Žižek; Jameson 1991, xvii). Put slightly differently, this transaesthetic vector points toward the arrival of what Lukács called the subject-object of history—the proletariat—or Hegel's absolute spirit, an equally contentious sublation of the subject/object division, both of these material or ideal overcomings of oppositions. In this sense modernism is utopian, intimating the world to come; and in this sense, modernism's agon over the single and the multiple leads to a thinking of how the future might derive from the present.

But Theodor Adorno, who will be much in evidence here, possesses a healthy allegiance to the *bilderverbot*, and for him there is no room in art or thought for images of a reconciled future, regardless of materialist or idealist inflection, images that can only be as impossible—or as false—as they are desirable. And yet, in one of his most quoted passages, he writes this: "The only philosophy which can be responsibly practiced in the face of despair is the attempt to contemplate all things as they would present themselves from the standpoint of redemption. Knowledge has no light but that shed on the world by redemption . . . Perspectives must be fashioned that displace and estrange the world, reveal it to be, with its rifts and crevices, as indigent and distorted as it will appear one day in the messianic light" (Adorno 1974, 247).

There is much we could discuss about this remarkable passage, but I will restrict myself to two points, one blindingly obvious and one a little less so, hopefully. First, here, as in so much of his thought, Adorno reveals himself as an heir to the Enlightenment and even Romanticism, as the light that the impossible perspective of redemption provides will never be called upon to shine up and reveal the face of God but, pointedly, is invoked to reveal the damaged world below—not the world to come, but the world, finally, as it is. Attendant here is a conception of thought not as that which subsumes the object, leaving no remainder, but rather as that which finally, impossibly, *reveals* the object. But second, his linking of light with redemption offers a half-rhyme with the thought of a contemporary of his, with whom we may be forgiven for thinking the German philosopher had little enough in common. It is André Bazin, film theorist and founder of *Cahiers du Cinéma*, anti-Marxist and Catholic, for whom the light passing through the lens and onto the emulsion, the light pouring from the projector and reflected by the screen, promises redemption. In his essay "The Ontology of the Photographic Image," Bazin argues that cinema is—or rather can be—objectivity in time, "change mummified." A film as a product of mechanical and technological reproduction gives the medium a privileged relation to the real, enabling it to grasp and preserve the real as if without the intervention of a troublesome—interested, limited—subjectivity. And it is this privileged relation, this technical objectivity, that informs what he names the "mummy complex": an ancient yet intrinsic human desire to step out of time and preserve the moment and duration, the object, real space, and redeem it in and as the image. "Redeem" because every film and photograph potentially bears endless witness to the beauty of God's creation, a beauty so generous and multiple that it risks being lost without these singular, mechanical traces of its miraculous being and transience (Bazin 1967, 9–16).

It is surely easy enough to criticize Bazin's explicit program, but any of us with a smart phone and a child or cute pet should probably think twice. More profitable, I think, would be to consider the relation between Bazin and Adorno, to ask after the relationship between the image and its object. Adorno writes, "Duration of the transient, an element of art that at the same time perpetuates the mimetic heritage, is one of the categories that dates back to primeval times . . . [T]he image itself . . . is one of regeneration . . . Yet it is apparent that precisely in the early history the achievement of duration was accompanied by consciousness of its futility, perhaps even that such duration—in the spirit of the prohibition on graven images—was tied up with a sense of guilt toward the living" (Adorno 1997, 280). As in Bazin, art here for Adorno suggests that resemblance—mimesis—is in the service of preservation, a desire to interrupt the flow of history itself and bring the past into the present that it might seem regenerated, its pulse might throb again and not remain merely past, inert, and dead. But unlike Bazin (and shades of *Totem and Taboo*!), for Adorno such mummification brings not redemption but guilt. The "mummy complex" loses its innocence: "One of the models of art may be the corpse in its transfixed and imperishable form. In that case, the reification of the formerly living would date back to primordial times, as did the revolt against death as a magical nature-bound practice" (Adorno 1997, 281). Art preserves—reifies—the dead at the cost of the guilt of the living, who must then invoke the ban on images to manage that guilt, which is not solely survivor's guilt but also the guilt that inheres in the willful alchemy of transforming subjects into aesthetic objects, essentially a second murder of the already dead. Thus art derives, too, from sacrifice, as this repetition of death entails the surrender of the dead and their deliverance into the second death of art, their singularity sacrificed so that they might persist as art. This transubstantiation of the dead is also mirrored in the fetish that precedes art, offering a magical connection between the material and its representation. For the fetish must be metonymic rather than mimetic or metaphorical—the doll must include human hair if it is to function—and so the object might persist in and finally by means of its representation. But at the same time, sacrifice and the fetish hint at what is to come: "What is done to the spear, the hair, the name of the enemy, is also to befall his person; the sacrificial animal is slain in the place of the god. The substitution which takes place in sacrifice marks a step towards discursive logic" (Adorno and Horkheimer 2002, 6). Sacrifice, magic, and the fetish may come to lead to what is here labeled discursive logic, but what stands behind that is identity thinking itself, the reduction and imprisonment of subject and object both by the concept. And yet art sits only ambivalently amid this fraught constellation. Deriving from sacrifice, magic, and fetishism it nonetheless remains distinct, even coming to use elements from these to its own ends: "Although magical fetishes are one of the historical roots of art, a fetishistic element remains admixed in artworks, an element that goes beyond commodity fetishism" (Adorno 1997, 227). Crucially, and not incidentally, this will entail for Adorno a refigured concept of mimesis in art, which will in turn demand not this literal preservation or mirror-image identity but rather a playful and nonrepressive transformation of the object in the image—that is, the image, art, shifts from expressing its identity with its object, and thus its guilt-inspiring dominance over it, and becomes something more symbolic—more autonomous.

If for Adorno art's preservation of the dead entails the guilt of the living that then entails the birth of a mimesis more playful than exact, for Bazin the preservation of the dead, as well as that of the object and real time, demands of the image a scrupulous and exact fidelity to its object. He writes, "If the history of the plastic arts is less a matter of their aesthetic than of their psychology then it will be seen to be essentially the story of resemblance, or, if you will, of realism" (Bazin 1967, 9). Indeed, one of the most striking points that Bazin will make has to do not just with the affinity of the apparatus with the objects of the world but with how this affinity seems to afford to us nothing less than the fulfillment of phenomenology: "Now, for the first time, the image of things is likewise the image of their duration, change mummified, as it were" (Bazin 1967, 15). The image coincides with its object; and indeed Bazin will go on to claim that the image itself is as unique and natural as any object it takes up—images are as natural and thing-like as snowflakes, in his own memorable image. Now we would surely have good reason to ask after the extent to which any film or photograph might truly be an unmediated apprehension of its object; but what might be most radical about Bazin's claim is this possibility of grasping objects as they are in themselves, apart from the web of perception and consciousness—as they are, perhaps, to God. For Bazin cinema answers the call.

What is at stake here, and what effectively links Bazin with Adorno, is the thinking of a noncoercive relationship between the image and its object—which is another way of expressing a desire for a noncoercive relationship between subject and object. From absence and presence to the one and the multiple to the future and the present; from the living and the dead to the subject and the object, all these oppositions necessarily impinge on our thinking about art and film.

These oppositions and contradictions are only apparently opposed at all. This is not necessarily to say, as in deconstruction, for example, that the priority of the single over the multiple harbors a secret and suspicious metaphysics; nor is it to say that the divide between the living and the dead is to be overcome in a crude dialectical sublation. This *is* to say that these oppositions must be both true *and* false: as Adorno writes of the subject and object's separation, "[t]rue, because in the cognitive realm it serves to express the real separation, the dichotomy of the human condition, a coercive development. False, because the resulting separation must not be hypostatized, not magically transformed into an invariant" (Adorno 1998, 246). That is, descriptively the separation of subject and object is true, and not just in terms of Bazin's sense of our isolation from the object-world that we desire to overcome with film, but also cognitively, in that our concepts are never identical to the object, just as the object always falls short of our conception of it. Thought and the object do not meet without producing remainders on either side; and it is precisely these remainders that bespeak the falsity of a rationality that is normative, that assumes that the subject's concept might be equal to the object, that the two correspond—which is really a cover for the subject's dominance of the object. Thus "[t]he only way to make out objectivity is to reflect, at each historic and each cognitive step, on what is then presented as subject and object, as well as on the mediations" (Adorno 1998, 253). We might do worse than to take this for a description of Adorno's critical program as such.

Film fits only ambiguously within the modernist program I've sketchily outlined here. It offers works that it is inarguably useful to think of as singular, that seek to include or trump all other examples, as in Godard's delirious, encyclopedic *Histoire(s) du cinéma* (1988–98), an ambitious attempt to "sublate" the medium itself as a kind of class of all classes; or alternately his *Weekend* (1967), which announces "*La fin du cinéma,*" a critical gesture that aims to negate the medium's history in the hope that political praxis might replace consumption. However, such filmic examples must always struggle to assert their singularity over and against their status as film—that is, as mechanically reproduced and irreducibly multiple when not utter commodities. Walter Benjamin's "The Work of Art in the Age of its Technical Reproducibility" aims to solve this problem by way of offering a genealogy of this singularity itself, now labeled *aura* and no longer specifically modernist but rather revealed to be a real illusion, an illegitimate claim of transcendence that masks a history of ritual, discipline, mystification, and manipulation (Benjamin 2002). Aura, less a quality of the work itself, is to be conceived as supplied by the disciplinary and institutional contexts that come to house the work, pointedly to keep it at a distance from the masses, who in their turn can only come to it in reverence or puzzlement if at all. Alternately, for Benjamin, new forms such as film promise the possibility of a more critical approach to the work of art, with consciousness and perception no longer taxed by distance, under the spell of the aura: brought close, the work must submit to a dispassionate gaze of an audience in distraction.

This essay, though, in the authority it still possesses in film and media studies, radiates an aura of its own, and this despite its otherwise tireless if finally ambivalent undoing of the aura as disciplinary and mystifying. This is to wonder after the extent to which modern and modernist texts, a rubric under which we surely must include Benjamin and Beckett, both possess an aura *and* depend utterly upon their technical reproducibility, existing in innumerable copies, separate from their origins, eluding the division of the manual and the technical and so on, such that, while meeting the criteria Benjamin establishes for the technically reproduced work, *Godot*'s text and performances cannot be said to be lacking in aura. And so Benjamin's own text—how distant does it now seem?—itself comes to be characterized by an aura, which, if not the product of the mystifications of church or state, derives from the failure of film to be what he hoped—finally, we must suspect, a problem of the essay as much as the medium.[2]

For film it seems more productive to consider this dialectic of modernism and mass culture in terms of the necessary relationship between aesthetic technique and industrial technology, particularly in that film's dependence on industrial technology (as a means of reproduction and circulation) dominates aesthetic technique (as the internal organization of aesthetic material) in a manner distinct from earlier aesthetic modes and forms. For Adorno, again in opposition to Bazin, film as an industrial technology that permits that seemingly objective and redemptive capture of the object-world is constraining in at least two respects: first, its ties to an indexicality or an older mimesis can only be felt as limiting, compromising the artist's freedom and the possibility of an absolute construction; and second, in its blurring of the former distinction between technique and technology, film comes to side with what Adorno identifies as the inherent tendencies of all technology—that is, the domination of nature. Again, to differentiate this from Bazin, for Adorno the indexical or iconic image under modernity may make for good theology (though that is a loaded question), but it can now only make for bad art, as it limits the artist to that older aesthetic mode of realism while simultaneously concealing a covert agenda—the domination of nature, an assertion of the sovereign distinction between subject and object—even as technology and its attendant rationality makes film a thing among other things: a commodity, not a snowflake.

But Adorno's characterization of technology, particularly in the contexts of art and film, has another aspect, too: for it falls upon art to try to repair the damages wrought by industrial technology and its attendant modes of thought—this is how and why art must be modern. But what does this mean? It is clearly not enough merely to represent on the level of content the world of technology and its attendant effects of the sub-ject, the social, and nature, for this would only reify technol-ogy as a second nature, an inveterate given rather than part of the problem to be addressed; and neither, as I've suggested, is the solution to be found on a formal level, in which art might come to mimic the rhythms of industrial production—most film does this already, with predictable enough results. Nei-ther strategy could acknowledge the subjective dimension of this objectifying of the industrial-technological world, as the focus on content implies the pernicious separation of subject and object, while the form asserts an oppressive identity between the industrial world and the subject. That these are both part of the same tendency, which Adorno famously refers to as the dialectic of enlightenment, can be demonstrated by that text's thesis, in which the domination of (outer) nature tends to include the domination of inner nature—subjectivity—as well.

To put it slightly differently, art's problems with the par-ticular and the multiple, the subject and the object, stem from the sense in which the former opposition of subject and object has now been overcome, though not in Hegel's or Marx's sense—that is, to keep it in the context of film, subjects, viewers, and audience have been reduced to objects, points of consumption, by the films' technology that, having mastered outer nature, now disfigures the inner; while in its status as commodity, like all commodities it has assumed an uncanny life of its own, stolen from the now invisible labor that constituted it. Alternately, to consider the subject as simply—even naively—separate from the world accurately reflects the subject's desire to master the world while simultaneously being alienated from it, even as such a consideration is false to the extent that it *naturalizes* this separation and alienation, prescribing it as the limit of our engagement with the world. Therefore art—here film—must find another approach: it must stress the *primacy* of the object in order to avoid both the dominating tendencies and the domination of the subject.

Aesthetic experience is not to be understood as the subject's experience of the object but rather as that which constitutes the crisis of the identity of subject and object—aesthetic experience shifts the goalposts, compelling us to question our relationship to the object, which is never ready-at-hand or strictly an in-itself, always both with and without aura. And *The Maltese Falcon* (1941) offers an opportunity to question our relation to the film and the object. If "[t]he separation of subject and object is both real and semblance" (Adorno 1998, 246), then here film might come to provide an evident mediation between the two without compelling this opposition to ossify into an invariant or ideology; it might come to displace a conception of the subject as that which "swallows object, forgetting how much it is object itself" (Adorno 1998, 246); and it may finally attempt an approach to the object that can more fully countenance its otherness, its complexity, its noumenal wealth—that is, "[k]nowledge of the object is brought closer by the act of the subject rending the veil it weaves about the object" (Adorno 1998, 254). Such a program is at once epistemological, aesthetic, and political.

The Maltese Falcon does appear singular in many respects: it's often thought of as one of the first film noirs (but then that "one of" immediately qualifies its singularity); it was Bogart's first heroic leading role and John Huston's first director's credit; and it is, of course, about a fabulously singular object, the Falcon itself, of which more in a minute. Then again, it was the third adaptation of Dashiell Hammet's novel, following *The Maltese Falcon* (1931), also known as *Dangerous Female* (1931) directed by Roy Van Ruth, and *Satan Met a Lady* (1936), directed by William Dieterle. No fewer than three *Falcons* in ten years—Hollywood's penchant for remakes has a long history, the distinction here being that these earlier *Falcons* were pretty unsuccessful, and the last did not seek to ride the coattails of an earlier generation's blockbuster as contemporary remakes seem to wish to. But the second of these remains a distinctive if somewhat schizoid affair: part pre–Hays Code and therefore sexy screwball comedy, part murder mystery, as a thing of parts it offers something for everyone and so might seem finally to possess less of an identity itself. And yet maybe this proliferation of *Falcons* also serves to suggest Huston's *Falcon's* singularity, as the only one most of us can be bothered to remember anymore.

Why do we remember it, if indeed we do? A good deal of the film's appeal hinges on our identification with Bogart's Sam Spade, an identification that the detective genre promotes in a very particular manner. The detective's interpretation of events, along with his desire or willingness to assign guilt or innocence, effectively mirrors our engagement, as we sift the scene for clues and come to judge motive and character—his command of reflective judgment mirrors and models our own. The detective makes clear what seems opaque, as insignificant material traces will be compelled to surrender meaning—those traces will be redeemed—and he redeems the crimes of the past with the promise of justice—or at least knowledge—in the future. As identification shades into eschatology, the detective thus possesses a redemptive and utopian role analogous to that I evoked earlier for modernism, a role perhaps not too distant from Adorno's own, as the detective's perspective lights upon a "bright and guilty world" (to borrow from Welles's *The Lady from Shanghai* [1947]), and reveals it finally as meaningful. And in a related sense, to which we will return, the detective finds himself ambiguously positioned between the law and the criminal world, beholden to neither but resolutely, impossibly subjective and free. He is at the merest remove from the world as it is, but in film at least this is enough of a foothold for thought.

Except for the extent to which, as we are so often told, the private detective must abide by an individual code, one privileged over and against the inauthenticities of the law and the criminal worlds alike, which come to be disparaged, one assumes, for their social and collective status. This seems most in evidence here in Spade's final exchange with femme fatale Brigid O'Shaunessy (Mary Astor):

> SPADE. Listen. This won't do any good. You'll never under-
> stand me, but I'll try once and then give it up. When a
> man's partner is killed, he's supposed to do something. It
> makes no difference what you thought of him. He was
> your partner, and you're supposed to do something about
> it . . . and it happens we're in the detective business. Well,
> when one of your organization gets killed, it's . . . it's
> bad business to let the killer get away with it . . . bad all
> around, bad for every detective everywhere . . .
>   If all I've said doesn't mean anything to you then forget
> it and we'll make it just this: I won't, because all of me
> wants to regardless of consequences, and because you've
> counted on it, the same as you counted on it with all the
> others.

Spade here sacrifices his object (if I may put it that way), to assert his own private, subjective code of values. But is this the case? Does he send her over to pay a debt to a part-ner he hated, because he can't trust her, because it's bad for business, bad all round? What would it mean to suggest that Spade's sacrifice, rather than being ethical, hews closer to self-preservation, with the sacrifice of his object of desire substi-tuting for his desire itself, serving to affirm and armor the self? Reality, the object—what the woman is reduced to—is mastered, while the purpose of a mastery—the satisfaction of the self—is thus squandered in the service of maintaining a subjectivity that becomes increasingly thing-like and dead, as thing-like as Brigid turns out to be in this sacrificial drama. In seeking to preserve himself as subject, in sacrificing Brigid as an object, Spade becomes an object himself.

The ethical hero of *The Maltese Falcon*, indeed the detective as such, comes to instantiate a figure that is at once classical and modern and thus paradoxically confirms the contrapuntal historicity of the dialectic of enlightenment itself, as myth becomes enlightenment and enlightenment reverts to myth. For Spade here looks like Adorno's Odysseus: if this classical hero is transformed into a traveling salesman on a business trip in Adorno and Horkheimer's text, it is then dialectically necessary to complement the redemptive vocation I earlier ascribed to the detective figure with a similar critique. Odysseus, the first bourgeois subject, allows himself to be bound so that he may hear the Sirens' song, and Spade's ethics seem no less effective than the ropes that fasten Odysseus to the phallic mast in keeping him from an alluring feminine threat, one that like the Sirens appears poised to test the certainties of the masculine ego and the limits of masculine ethics and to reveal the link between these two. For Adorno the Sirens appear as both nature and art, or rather nature then art; for when Odysseus can no longer be threatened by them, they become mere objects for contemplation and aesthetic judgment, decorous but dead.[3] And Odysseus at a stroke transforms from a heroic and intrepid leader to an emotional concertgoer, at the same time that his triumph over threatening and feminine nature is won at the cost of triumph over himself, his own submission to a self-imposed bondage:

> His comrades, who themselves cannot hear, know only the danger of the song, not of its beauty, and leave him tied to the mast to save both him and themselves. They reproduce the life of the oppressor as a part of their own, while he cannot step outside his social role. The bonds by which he has irrevocably fettered himself to praxis at the same time keep the Sirens at a distance from praxis: their lure is neutralized as a mere object of contemplation, of art. The fettered man listens to a concert, as immobilized as audiences later, and his enthusiastic call for liberation goes unheard as applause. (Adorno and Horkheimer 2002, 26–27)

But wily Odysseus also separates pleasure from work for his sailors, and henceforth for them art will be remote, a remoteness whose measure cannot be described by the aura but is rather to found in the gulf between the working and managerial classes, proletariat and bourgeoisie, and manual and abstract labor themselves. This is "objective spirit" and the beginning of what Adorno will come to call the administered world: the reason that characterizes objective spirit objectifies human relations, naturalizing Odysseus as administrator, the sailors as alienated workers, and the Sirens as the feminine made passive nature and even "art," this last burdened with something like all Plato's disdain for women and poetry both in the *Republic*. In this sense objective spirit is instrumental reason, allowing for the domination of both workers and nature and also of women as nature. Objective spirit administers— objective spirit takes the fingerprints of that critical spirit we wish to preserve and cultivate. Spade's sacrifice of Brigid, a sacrifice demanded by his ethics, but also by his fealty to business, stands explicitly against his own desire—"because all of me wants to"—and so the ultimate sacrifice here is of his own desire, happiness, and fulfillment, which stand revealed as victims not of ethics but of business, of an objective spirit that dominates him: in dominating Brigid he comes to participate in his own domination. And in this asymmetrical exchange, the specificity of what is lost in sacrifice—Brigid, happiness—might also be described as the sacrifice of specificity itself, entailing the validation of the principle of exchange as the only specificity recognized now.

But is Spade better with things than women, especially with that particular object that gives the film its title? We can begin to explore this by suggesting that Spade is no Holmes— Holmes, whose esoteric and encyclopedic knowledge could only ever affirm that the truth was, finally, accessible, that there was a possible relationship between subject and object, the self and the world. Holmes is undisputed master over material traces and subjective rationality—in a sense he is the dialectic of enlightenment externalized, an embodiment of the mastery of nature as well as the mastery of subjectivity, not exempting his own—really, he has no desire beyond cocaine. But Bogart's Spade is something else, for he carries no magnifying glass. His interest is not with the objects of the world, forlorn traces that bespeak guilt; rather—and this is the ultimate seal of our identification with this particular figure—his allegiance is primarily with narrative, even history, if we wish to think of history as narrative. When Brigid O'Shaunessy revises an earlier story of her own—that she was hiring Spade and Archer to search for her missing and nonexistent sister—Spade replies, "Oh that—we didn't believe your story, we believed your $200." To Spade it matters little that the story is untrue: what matters is that its untruth is paid for, redeemed by money, redeemed by abstract exchange. Stories here are subject to the laws of exchange, value, and negotiation—stories, we might as well say art, need not refer to the world in an exact and scrupulous manner to have value; they need not be indexical or mimetic in that older sense. Rather it is through exchange, even here through the commodification of narrative, that their only value can be found. And yet at the same time, despite their circulation and valuation in economic terms, stories may also allow a more playful and mimetic approach to the objects they seek to explore. It is useful to contrast Gutman's story of the Falcon with Brigid's story as well as Spade's own. For Kasper Gutman (Sydney Greenstreet) the value of the black bird is indissociable from its history, which he usefully recaps for us:

> GUTMAN. What do you know of the Order of the Hospital of Saint John of Jerusalem, later known as the Knights of Rhodes?
> SPADE. Crusaders or something, weren't they?
> GUTMAN. Very good. Sit down. These crusading Knights persuaded Emperor Charles V to give them the Island of Malta. He made but one condition: that they pay him yearly the tribute of a falcon in acknowledgement that Malta was still under Spain. Do you follow me? Have you any conception of the extreme, the immeasurable wealth of the Order of that time?
> SPADE. They were pretty well fixed.
> GUTMAN. "Pretty well" is putting it mildly. They were rolling in wealth, sir. For years they'd taken from the East nobody knows what spoils of gems, precious metals, silks, ivory, sir. We all know the Holy Wars to them were largely a matter of loot. The Knights were profoundly grateful to the Emperor Charles for his generosity toward them. They

hit upon the thought of sending for his first year's tribute, not an insignificant live bird but a glorious golden falcon, crusted from head to foot with the finest jewels in their coffers . . . These are facts, historical facts, not schoolbook history, not Mr. Wells' history, but history, nevertheless. They sent the foot-high jeweled bird to Charles in Spain. They sent it in a galley commanded by a member of the Order. It never reached Spain. A famous admiral of buccaneers took the Knights' galley and the bird. It turned up in Sicily. It appeared in Paris. It had, by that time, acquired a coat of black enamel, so that it looked nothing more than a fairly interesting black statuette.

The Crusades promised nothing less than enlightenment—Christianity, over the "myths" of the East—and revealed themselves as domination. On one level the Falcon's and Gutman's are stories of reversals and failed exchanges: crusades become plunder, an island is traded for a falcon that never arrives, and a jeweled falcon for a live one. The Falcon is priceless, beyond exchange, fabulously singular—in its particular being whole histories of violence, murder, theft, and domination coalesce. A product of a bloody history, it seeks to transcend history, to cancel or redeem all the violence that attended its coming into being. Here value flows from the historical narrative of the Crusades to guarantee the object, the Falcon, as priceless. Or, if you prefer, Gutman is the Holmes figure here, elaborating a narrative of the past that confers meaning in the present—not just meaning, but also value, even redemption, and especially his own, as he hopes possession of the Falcon will make good the 17 years devoted to tracing clues of its elusive presence. But as the film allows him to recount this history, the history of the Falcon and the history of his search and so his history, it will also trace his historical passing away, along with the belief that the narrative—history, even rationality—guarantees the object's truth and being, which the narrative moves swiftly to undo.

With Spade it proceeds precisely in reverse:

CAIRO. I shouldn't think it necessary to remind you that you may have the falcon, but we certainly have you.

SPADE. I'm trying not to let that worry me. We'll get back to
the money later on. There's something else to be discussed
first. We've got to have a fall guy. The police need a victim,
somebody they can pin those three murders on.
CAIRO. Three? There's only two, because Thursby certainly
killed your partner.
SPADE. Only two then. What's the difference?

Now for Spade money is no longer a pressing issue or consideration in the forging of narrative, no longer a guarantee that
a narrative will serve its function—and this when narrative
is called upon to account for murder: three or two, "What's
the difference?" What are the stakes for narrative then if not
money and exchange? if murder is negligible and guilt or
innocence irrelevant? The presence of the mythic bird in all
its value is not the end of the story but now the beginning of
another, as Spade uses it to guarantee the story to come, the
one to be told the police, who evidently have need of stories,
too: Wilmer (Elisha Cook Jr.), the gunsel, is the murderer;
his motive jealousy or greed, it hardly matters; his weapon
his gun. Here the object guarantees the story, and Gutman,
O'Shaunessy, Wilmer, and Cairo (Peter Lorre) must accept it,
false as it is, because Spade possesses the Falcon. What matters
here is less that these narrative inventions will be set right in
the end, with Spade reaffirming his ethical status, but rather
that finally he can only accomplish this by means of this story
and the Falcon that affirms it, that makes it possible, and is its
very origin and occasion.

Here again Spade seems a modern Odysseus, wily, rational.
This particular narrative invention, near the end of the film,
has already been signaled at several points by Spade's penchant for manipulation and deception: his affair with Ida, his
partner's wife; his feigning anger at an earlier meeting with
Gutman and Wilmer; and his invention of an outrageous
story to mollify the police when Cairo and O'Shaunessy
come to blows in his apartment. It is then on the side of the
subject that we have located the use and value of narrative,
through these considerations of O'Shaunessy, Gutman, and
Spade. But these last two affirm the value and power of narrative in terms of the presence or absence of the titular Falcon
itself, which must call for a shift of gears; for if the Falcon can

seemingly ambivalently be called upon to redeem history or rewrite history, we will need then to think of it as a very special kind of object indeed, one whose being is not exhausted by the disparate uses to which it is put.

To think of narrative from the side of the object might not yet be to accord to it its proper and fulsome being—that will have to wait—but to wonder after what might make it amenable to its deployment and motivation in these contradictory narrative contexts. We can enumerate some of these qualities: Gutman ties it to a material history, but its very being and materiality are mythic and vague, and ultimately what we are shown is a fake; and Spade cares less about its materiality or even truth, it seems, than the dingus's ability to act as an anchor for the narratives he spins. Following this last we can add that in its function as a guarantee of the efficacy of his discourse, the seal of its performativity, the Falcon thus acts as a fulcrum around which the shifting network of allegiances among the group come to turn—not just narrative then, the Falcon also comes to structure the social. But to call the Falcon a dingus as Spade does already provides an answer: the *Oxford English Dictionary* (*OED*) defines *dingus* as "a thing one cannot or does not wish to name specifically." Such a signifier applied to the Falcon appears to recognize that there is more to it than it seems, an elusive or threatening being beyond its name; and this definition also usefully confirms that its being exists as if beneath a veil or under a ban, marked by desire and prohibition. But this is then *das ding*:[4]

> *Das Ding* is that which I will call the beyond-of-the-signified. It is as a function of this beyond-of-the-signified and of an emotional relationship to it that the subject keeps its distance and is constituted in a kind of relationship characterized by primary affect, prior to any repression . . .
>
> It remains for us to see that it is in the same place that something which is the opposite, the reverse and the same combined, is also organized, and which in the end substitutes itself for the dumb reality which is *das Ding*—that is to say, the reality that commands and regulates. That is something that emerges in the philosophy of someone who, better than anyone else, glimpsed the function of *das Ding*, although he only approached it by the

path of the philosophy of science namely, Kant. (Lacan 1992,
54–55)

As with the Falcon, *das ding* in its specificity remains stubbornly outside symbolization and so at a distance from the
subject, who nonetheless remains tied to it via "an emotional
relationship" and a "primary affect," with the opposition
between its motivation through competing narratives now
revealed as its ineluctability, as finally it circulates in and out
of the reality to which it is both opposed and "the same."
The issue of affect is crucial, though, and will be raised by
Lacan in an astonishing paragraph describing Harpo Marx,
who instantiates *das ding* by virtue of his dumbness, his status
outside signification and the Symbolic themselves: "Is there
anything that poses a question which is more present, more
pressing, more absorbing, more disruptive, more nauseating,
more calculated to thrust everything that takes place before us
into the abyss or void than that face of Harpo Marx, that face
with its smile which leaves us unclear as to whether it signifies
the most extreme perversity or complete simplicity?" (Lacan
1992, 55).[5] More than merely resting beyond signification
das ding maintains a disruptive presence within it, provoking
extremes of affect and posing a crisis for signification as such.
For Lacan this results ambivalently in fascination and nausea,
though we could also pause to cite another example: John
Carpenter's *The Thing* (1982), which disrupts, in graphic and
unsettling ways, whole modes of scientific thought, producing terror and ultimately breaking down the Symbolic consis-
tency of identity and even bodies themselves.

Although little enough of this extreme affect seems available in Huston's film, the Falcon itself does find ways to unset-
tle all the same. When it finally and fatally arrives at Spade's
office, dropped from the dead hands of Captain Jacoby, his
self-composure is tested:

> SPADE. We've got it, Angel! We've got it!
> [Laughing, he puts his arms around Effie, crushing her body
>   against his]
> EFFIE. You're hurting me!

Figure 1.1   Effie and Sam unwrap the Falcon

While not the full-blown crisis that Harpo's face seems to evoke, laughter and unconscious violence together announce the ambivalent affect brought about by the proximity of *das ding*. And yet *das ding*'s status as the "beyond-of-the-signifier" can only fit oddly within a film that names itself after its figure here, among a group of characters all in pursuit of it, and within a series of sequences and frames so seemingly eager to grasp it, to conjure it into being and fulsome presence. Both external and internal to representational protocols and the desire to integrate it within the Symbolic, it comes to be registered as a kind of crisis and symptom for the subject, and even perhaps the film itself, the symptom at once a signifier and an enigmatic question, a "message from the real" as Lacan will suggest.[6]

From here we could follow Lee Edelman's implacable tracking of the *das ding* in its circulation, coming to note its function as an ambiguous "thing-presentation" anterior to representation and as that which will come to be condensed in and as the figure of the phallus itself (Edelman 1994). But the Falcon, now as phallus, also confirms the detective's affiliation to the law in the way it authorizes a policing of sexuality: thus everyone desires the phallus/Falcon, but their relation to it is to be determined by the central figure, heteronormative and masculine. So to the ensemble of queers the film proffers—the exotic Cairo, the decadent Gutman, and the gunsel Wilmer—it is to be denied, while the femme fatale's play for the phallus must result in her destruction or containment. What Spade seems to sense that they do not and what also authorizes and enables his use of the Falcon to anchor his stories and now actions would then be an awareness of its status, precisely, as signifier: that is, not something that can be possessed or embodied—that would be the phallus in the Imaginary—but rather something to be used in the Symbolic itself, to anchor the chain of signification now conceived not just in terms of language but also in terms of social and sexual relations. But in these terms then masculinity itself loses its longed-for essence, as it can only be affirmed negatively, against feminine and queer sexuality, abetted by its Symbolic supplement.

Moreover, if indeed the Falcon comes to underwrite this task for the detective—the policing of the borders of sexuality—then we might also return this figure of the detective to another history: not the eschatological one of the redemption of meaning and promise of justice, though, as Spade creates meaning only continually to affirm his privileged access to the Symbolic phallus, and though O'Shaunessy, Gutman, Cairo, and Wilmer all may be criminals, "justice" now seems to be an alibi for Spade's treatment of these. That this psychic drama is also necessarily social authorizes the other history I offer now. Walter Benjamin writes, "Preformed in the figure of the *flâneur* is that of the detective. The *flâneur* required a social legitimation of his habitus. It suited him very well to see his indolence presented as a plausible front, behind which, in reality, hides the riveted attention of an observer who will not let the unsuspecting malefactor out of his sight" (Benjamin 1999, 442). It would seem that in the hard-boiled detective's assertion of what will constitute the "proper" in sexuality, the *flâneur*'s social legitimation has indeed been found, and the crowds over and against which he asserts his distinction and covertly maintains his liminal status come to be feminized and criminal all at once. And similarly, if the arcades announce with their covered streets and broad shop windows a blurring of the boundaries of public and private space in the service of consumption, then necessarily the detective/*flâneur*'s interest in criminals as well as his interest in "distinction"—the cut of one's clothes, the physiognomy of a face—bespeak an interest in things, in commodities, even in the feminized crowd itself reduced to a dazzling, spectacular commodity, reflected kaleidoscopically in the mirrors and shop windows that line the arcades. From this perspective the *flâneur* looks more like the mall security guard, though perhaps better dressed; but now it is his attentiveness to things to which we must attend, an interest born of his nearly phenomenological reduction of the social into glittering and guilty objects.[7] His singularity is affirmed in this covert form, while the individuals that comprise the crowd become ultimately fungible.

The *flâneur*'s gaze is an aesthetic and an aestheticizing one and one that for Benjamin is absolutely modern in its promotion of this discriminating gaze via the quantitative expansion of exchange and the commodity form into spheres from which they were at one time, presumably, distinct. *Reification* describes this process, as social relations and living bodies come to appear thing-like and dead. It seems no longer an issue for the *flâneur* to worry after the crowd or commodity as they might be in themselves—as they might appear outside this phantasmagoria of exchange. And as for the *flâneur* so for the detective, whose ties to the material world, to the redemption of chaos through the deliverance of meaning, wither, to be replaced by a more instrumental and reductive gaze. Such a gaze arguably comes to be part and parcel of the experience of film itself, with our pleasure in distraction or our pleasure in a world rendered meaningful now corralled and determined as a pleasure in the living made dead and the object made merely functional when not wholly indifferent and exchangeable. The arcades open up as the cinema; the *flâneur* announces the coming of the Culture Industry, the production of calculated affect, the standardization of objects and subjects both, the coordination and synchronization of innumerable particulars into affirmative wholes, with the differences between or among the reified images as minimal as gaps between rival colas. This is a broad claim, but it is one, I hope, that derives from the covert itinerary I have been tracing, for the reification and commodification, self-preservation and self-sacrifice, and our original problematic of the single and the multiple all fall in line as examples of a broader tendency, whose name I have already evoked: the dialectic of enlightenment itself, that regression through progress. Adorno and Horkheimer relate a history that is the history of sacrifice, from the sacrifice of offerings to the gods, to the sacrifice of the self to business, to the sacrifice of the particularities of subject and object both the indifferent and ubiquitous principle of exchange.

To condense this, to constellate it in a form that might offer opportunities that otherwise seem unavailable, instead of a summary I can offer a narrative: art emerges from magic and the fetish, offering an ambivalent mimesis that attests to the real but thereafter comes to be entangled with its instrumentalization. In the shift from the sacrifice to the gods to the sacrifice of the self, it threatens to become merely decorative or functional, severed from nature, whether this last is conceived as external or internal. As identity thinking and especially exchange value dominate, art must resist the commodity or be subsumed by it. Historically art has been both victim and collaborator in this process—but it is not, for all that, identical with it. Indeed, Adorno's own focus on art, in a variety of forms and modes, from diverse historical periods, must then follow the same rhythm announced by the dialectic of enlightenment itself, under which progress, however longed for, also betrays the scars and marks of a regress, and older forms, no matter how rigorously they must be negated, are also subjected to a patient and penetrating scrutiny in the hope that there might persist traces of opportunities missed or discarded. And this last is particularly crucial for a modernism that seeks to "make it new" but might only do so through a patient and endless inventory of the old—a modernism that seeks to staunch the wounds inflicted upon countless particulars by the totalizing tendencies of its conjoined twin, the

Figure 1.2   The Falcon

Culture Industry, by attempting a monumental and impossible particularity itself.

But if this is a necessarily reductive history of the work of art, from its origins in magic and myth to its desperate bid for singularity, it is also a history that *The Maltese Falcon* (and the Maltese Falcon) exemplifies and rehearses. What then is the Falcon? It is an image of nature reified and mute, yet still an image of nature. It is an emblem of subjective domination: a tribute to a king, it comes covered in the blood of the dead, redolent of sacrifice. It is—and this is crucial—the figure of art itself, and for that, a dingus, as "art" is not to be mentioned in a commodity film, a genre film. It is an emblem of how film, or this film at least, comes to imagine another form of cultural value, desperately searching for terms other than its own with which to conceive of it, and so it emerges from history to transcend history, from film to transcend film, as timeless and placeless, and finally as mythic. It is a modernist monad; it is the book of the world. It is a riddle and enigma whose being shimmers on the cusp of materiality and ideality, whose very reality can only be in dispute, though not, for all that, its real effects. It is an absolute particular that resists conceptualization and commodification, that holds in reserve its innermost being all the while intimating it. It is auratic, wreathed by light, forever at a distance from all who seek it; it is threatened by banality in its very iteration, how it is submitted to affirm and account for the limits of desire, sexual or aesthetic. It is necessarily subject to exchange, its specificity challenged. It is a real fake, a necessary illusion, that comes to imply the redemption of illusion—though not yet, and not within the film. It is a bid for nonidentity; it is contradiction. It is how mass culture itself, in a way distinct from that of modernism, desires a totality, one that includes subject and object in a panoply of ways, that points toward a nonantagonistic relation between art and its other even while battening on that antagonism. It is how mass culture—pulp fiction, film noir—attempts to overcome the gap, at once real and ideological, that separates these two regimes of value and aesthetics, even as, finally, it points to the two as irreconcilable, "the torn halves of an essential freedom, to which, however, they do not add up" (Adorno and Benjamin 1999, 130).

We all remember, I think, the famous last line of the film—"The stuff that dreams are made of"—with which Sam Spade turns surprisingly Shakespearean in order to affirm the Falcon as an avatar of art, but also to affirm the difficulty, finally, of conceiving of a place for art within this world and this film, which, like Prospero, has come to abjure magic of that sort. Yet its dreamy being also conjures a utopian agenda—a future without want, a bloody past redeemed— that must be what disqualifies it from coming to a fuller presence here, as if such a promise must tactfully withdraw from further scrutiny—must, in order to keep faith with the suffering and conflict that has everywhere informed its very being, refuse to affirm what it is, or finally affirm very much at all. But Spade's is not the last word the film leaves us with—his response answers a question posed by the Detective Polhaus, who has asked, "What is it?," the very question that we have had. Polhaus has the last word, a word that does not appear in any script I have consulted but is there in the film in reply to Spade. Polhaus says, "Huh?" as the closing music begins to swell and the film ends. Something about the object remains a puzzle, opaque and inaccessible; something about Shakespeare, utopian aspirations, uncanny singular objects, and modernist art all withdraws from our ability to grasp it in its elusive being. At the end of the film it has excused itself into nonknowledge and nonbeing, into myth, in anticipation of another context and another time when its promise might be made good.

The Falcon then partakes of both Godot and the McGuffin, absent and present all at once. Its fundamental absence and dubious reality as scandalous as Godot's own, it likewise aims to put meaning and identity in crisis; and like the McGuffin, its presence and amenability to exchange promotes its use in a variety of instrumental and social contexts, which are then, we think, to be the real issues of concern for us as viewers—greed, perhaps, desire and sexuality, or ethics. But it is not a symbol, and it is not enough then even to suggest that this uncanny object has real effects, whether we think them to be ontological and existential or social and subjective. That it is the real McGuffin, mere pretext, the motivation of the device, and so on. For what is at stake here, what the film takes pains to render explicitly, is the extent to which this object, the Falcon, like all objects, like the film itself, like art, modernist and mass, finally withdraws from us, and in its withdrawal reveals itself to be something other or more than our idea of it or our instrumental use of it. This is in part Bazin's dream for cinema: that the object might be revealed in its plenitude, beyond its subjective apprehension. But as well, is it that, finally, the ontological status of the Falcon matters less than our approach to it, our noncoercive reflection on it that is invited and at stake, that remains the precondition for subjectivity as such? And *mutandis mutandi*, that the object never equals our (utopian) conception of it?

These questions are Adorno's, even if he would certainly object to the context from which I have tried to derive them, and likely to my conclusions, too. In the *Dialectic of Enlightenment* Adorno remotivates two crucial Hegelian concepts: determinate negation and conceptual self-reflection. This first begins as immanent critique:

The self-satisfaction of knowing in advance, and the transfig-
uration of negativity as redemption, are untrue forms of the
resistance to deception. The right of the image is rescued in the
faithful observance of its prohibition. Such observance, "determinate negation," is not exempted from the enticements of intuition by the sovereignty of the abstract concept, as is skepticism,
for which falsehood and truth are equally void. Unlike rigorism,
determinate negation does not simply reject imperfect representations of the absolute, idols, by confronting them with the idea
they are unable to match. Rather, dialectic discloses each image
as script. It teaches us to read from its features the admission
of falseness which cancels its power and hands it over to truth.
(Adorno and Horkheimer 2002, 18)

Again, this describes Adorno's method, but it is also one I have
tried to work through (helpfully the image presents itself here
and lends a foothold for film, even if that's not his context
in this place). If the Falcon—or any art or mode of thought
for that matter—gestures toward redemption, it cannot be
thought the opposite of deception but rather deception by
other means: an unearned affirmation that acts as a block to
further thought and so functions as mere ideology. In these
terms, then, the Falcon is true to the extent it does not appear
and cannot be affirmed—to the extent that it is sheerly negative, and not just toward the conditions or vagaries of its
image, but absolutely and utterly in terms of its context, to
be conceived of in the broadest terms possible, certainly of art
and film and also of the social and then of thought itself. For
it is not that this is an image of mere ideology or deception—
though it may be that, too—unequal to its concept and so
masking a fundamental social conflict or antagonism. It is a
script, another useful filmic term, which typically in Adorno
bears the weight of the prescriptive, determination and domination alike, but which here admits another reading. Indeed,
it *demands* another reading, a further reading—for its denunciation as false or ideological, while indispensable and as
always a testament to the necessity of the negative, is but a
step along the way to the wresting of truth from what seemed
only deception. Negative determination, then, would want

extravagantly to perform the script and push it past its prescriptive mandate such that its truth becomes evident.

Conceptual self-reflection entails both the need for concepts and vigilance toward them, demanding that we see them not as ends in and of themselves, or as hypostatized invariants, but always as derived from bodily desires and needs: "while real history is woven from real suffering, which certainly does not diminish in proportion to the increase in the means for abolishing it, the fulfillment of that prospect depends on the concept. For not only does the concept, as science, distance human beings from nature, but, as the self-reflection of thought—which, in the form of science, remains fettered to the blind economic tendency—it enables the distance which perpetuates injustice to be measured" (Adorno and Horkheimer 2002, 32). The concept is limiting: it is the very seal of identity thinking itself, the willful reduction of objects and experience by means of preexisting categories and the domination of outer and inner nature alike. Thought and the concept emerge for soma, from suffering and desire, and their alleged autonomy only renders those bodily experiences more distant. Therefore, first, the concept must be marshaled to testify to its adequacy to itself, to its own rootedness and origins in the body and its pains and pleasures, for it is ultimately in order to understand suffering that we cannot do without the concept. And here, I hope, the Falcon might also distantly evoke this trajectory, as from its abstraction it returns punctually to desire and its limits, out of a history of suffering and domination.

But conceptual self-reflection also implies another side to this remembrance, for its adequacy and even its truth can only be found in its eschewal of domination and its attempt to reconcile the human with nature—to imagine and enact a noncoercive relationship with the things of the world, not excepting other thinkers. As well as adequacy to its origins in bodily experience, then, conceptual self-reflection is necessarily a reflection on its adequacy to its object—an adequacy it seems impossible to achieve. For, like the Falcon, the object can only be arrested conceptually by way of its violent reduction by thought, a forceful cramming of it into a preexisting

schema that thus discards all its qualities that do not con-
form to the concept, qualities that now come to be labeled
as extraneous when not junk outright. This will be part of
what *Negative Dialectics* takes up. Itself a metacritique of
Kant, Hegel, and Heidegger and of the Idealist tradition as a
whole, it also insists that *all* thought needs be a metacritique
in order to avoid devolving into dogmatism and instrumen-
tality, in order to avoid doing violence to the object that was
its occasion. So the Kantian distinction between phenomena and noumena becomes suspect, since the transcendental
categories of experience are always marked by an experience
of a seemingly contingent materiality they are at pains to
contain. Genuine experience is constituted by precisely what
exceeds the a priori of the concept, the schema of the imagination. This scandalous excess, related to the noumenal, is
for Adorno the nonidentical.

And likewise the nonidentical marks the distance between
Adorno and Hegel; for while he shares Hegel's valuation of
speculative identity, Adorno insists that it has only ever been
achieved in a negative fashion; that the identity of subject and
object, or reason and reality, or even of that famous pair of
identity and nonidentity itself have indeed all been realized,
though not, alas, in the way Hegel would have wished. At
this end of the dialectic of enlightenment these identities and
others besides are produced by force, by the reductions of a
too narrow conceptual thought, but also by the sheer impress
of exchange value itself, under which the unlike must always
be finally alike.

Adorno's philosophy is thus a materialism, but never one
to sublate Kant or Hegel by fiat, and nowhere more so than
in what I have already raised in terms of the priority of the
object. Along with the attributes and strictures on thought I
have tried to summarize here, one of the most crucial for my
text will be this one: thought must honor the object, which
means thought must honor the nonidentical. It must come
agonizingly to grips with precisely that which presents the
most difficult challenges to identity thinking and the concept; it must seek to note and preserve precisely those aspects
of the object that exceed thought and the concept, those that

demand new concepts and better thought. It must painfully register that just as its own concepts derive from history and are not transcendent invariants, so, too, the object comes encrusted with its own history and so may and will change. The mode of thought that might do justice to the object and so also to itself is dialectics: "Contradiction is nonidentity under the aspect of identity; the dialectical primary of the principle of contradiction makes the thought of unity the measure of heterogeneity. As the heterogeneous collides with its limit it exceeds itself. Dialectics is the consistent sense of nonidentity" (Adorno 1973, 5). Finally, thought cannot do without identity—but that identity itself must come to be tirelessly tested for the heterogeneities and contradictions that it covers or elides, and only dialectics might grasp that nonidentity.

If such philosophical niceties appear arid and lifeless, we need only to think of the social itself, riven by antagonisms that are in turn papered over by ideologies or, almost worse, merely naturalized as "the way things are." Art, social through and through, bears the scars of both social antagonism and conceptual violence, but, at least in the modernist context that was Adorno's chief concern, it cannot permit itself merely to represent such contradictions without risking affirming them as given—and this is a risk even for art that seeks to engage and explicitly call for political change. Little is as easily commodified as dissent; but neither is this a reason to forgo wishing for a better world, which cannot come to be without imagining it first. "Insofar as a social function can be predicated for artworks, it is their functionlessness" (Adorno 1997, 227). Here from Kant and Marx alike art finds its vocation, its purposelessness now a rebuke to the abstractions of exchange value and conceptual thought both. Art is to be critical; it is to be negative. In its vocation to give body to an excess beyond exchange and beyond the concept it aims at truth not to be subsumed under pragmatics or correspondence. In its particularity and specificity beyond exchange it seeks to preserve that particularity as true and as truth—the truth then as what is first sacrificed under exchange.

Mostly for Adorno this relation to art and truth alike are denied film as a medium. The extent to which it is beholden to the industrial rhythms of production and technology, to the mechanical lockstep of the production of the ever-same, seem to disqualify it from ever being a modernist monad. But no one told *The Maltese Falcon*, which aims to be more than what it seems, which secretes within itself this kernel of nonidentity desperate never to be grasped or exchanged. This is to say that if *The Maltese Falcon* is not art—that it is rather a commodity, stylishly but traditionally produced for easy consumption, tiresomely repeating ideological messages about, say, the dangers of feminine and queer sexuality—then perhaps the Maltese Falcon is art; and therefore in retrospect what we will have witnessed is the film attempting to grope past that in it which is most affirmative—that says this is how films are made, this is what films do, this is how things are—toward its own kind of conceptual self-reflection. It tries to produce its own idea of the autonomous and particular even as it recognizes that that autonomy and particularity are denied it as a whole. The industrially produced and technologically reproduced film holds aloft this statuette, whose identity is so utterly self-contained and inviolate as to make Beckett appear voluble—but insofar as that identity, unstable and uncertain as it is, is the product of exploitation and bloodshed, it reflects back on the production of the film itself. Both film and statue are the products of differing modes of alienated labor; but only the Falcon, the film suggests, in its mythical and uncertain ontological status, can intimate a reconciliation to come. If the film can be reconciled with reality and history, the Falcon cannot and will not; and it remains an abstract and even dissonant element within the film's putative realism.[8]

CHAPTER 2

"A Deeper Breath"

From Body to Spirit in
Kiss Me Deadly (1955)

> For philosophy to be deep, a deep breath is called for.
> —Theodor Adorno, *Lectures on Negative Dialectics*

Kiss Me Deadly (dir. Robert Aldrich, 1955) gives us a world of venality, corruption, and sexual violence, a world in which greed and self-interest determine all relations. Programmatically, *Kiss Me Deadly* is a film about bodies: about the masculine body, construed as inviolate, and the feminine body, fatally permeable. It is therefore also a film about how and why the integrity of the masculine body will be maintained: it will be maintained by the repression of feminine sexuality, the repression of bisexuality, and the repression of homosexuality. Commodities will assert the power and integrity of this masculine body: cars, clothes, and technology are summoned to testify to the integrity of this body, its fulsomeness. This is, then, a *materialist* film, in both its content and its critical agenda. The film enacts a critique of how consumer culture functions to speak to and through the masculine ego and its gestalt; it is also materialist in its focus on the suffering consequent to this construal of the body, as brutality is punctually meted out upon other bodies. Bodies here labor, dance, suffer, and kiss. But if it is a film about the materiality of commodities and bodies, how they are subject to violence and exchange, then it is also a film about something *in excess* of the material that comes to possess flesh and goods—and film. One word for this excess is *spirit*; and to begin to think of what spirit might mean here, in the context of a world from which all positivity seemingly has been evacuated, we can look to how this film evinces an uncanny prescience in its grasp of how technologies of commodification and administration entangle and manage the spirit—and yet also come to evoke its reality. The voice negotiates this passage from body to spirit, material to ideal, even as it demonstrates the irreducibility of each of the pair to the other. The voice, always a privileged locus in film noir, will here do double duty. First, in its various relations to the body it will serve as an index of gendered power. But second, in its irreducibility to the body, it will lead past material bodies and things that seem so determinant here to assert, in a paradoxical sense that befits this film, the immanence of the immaterial: memory, art, spirit.

As I have discussed in the previous chapter, film for Theodor Adorno conforms all too readily to how things are. Depending as it does on industrial technology both in the capture of the object in front of the lens—thus stressing film's affinity with older aesthetic forms like realism, rather than modernism—and in its production and distribution, now in a commodified form, its industrial standards of rationality eliminate its difference from empirical existence, from the world of commodities. Film is affirmative—that is, film is too modern in its assumption of an industrial mode of production but not modern enough in its determinant ties to representation. Both of these tendencies decisively limit aesthetic autonomy.

Adorno insisted that his course lectures should *not* be published, even though they were recorded and transcribed. In an interview he says, "If I were to speak in the way that would be necessary to achieve the authority of a precise account I would be incomprehensible to my audience; nothing I say can do justice to what I demand from a text . . . The fact that everywhere today there is a tendency to record extempore speech and then to disseminate it is a symptom of the methods of the administered world which pins down the ephemeral word in order to hold the speaker to it. A tape recording is a kind of fingerprint of the living spirit" (Adorno 2001, 283). While we have already considered many of the aspects of film as a medium that he found compromised its status as art—its indexicality, its status as commodity—this quotation inflects those issues in another way, opening another horizon.

If film constrains aesthetic freedom and turns its objects into commodities, in this instance the tape-recorder "pins down the ephemeral word" like a specimen to hold the speaker accountable. Here the living spirit is not commodified but arrested, fingerprinted, perhaps even put in a lineup by the technologies of reproduction that serve to administer the world. This accounting that technology and administered society exact of the individual is to be sharply distinguished from justice, which is evoked by Adorno's desire in relation to the text. He must do justice to what he demands from the text, and this attempt must take the form of writing, of more text; thus his demand compels his accountability in a way that administered society would like to. Justice to the text must take the form of more text, but justice to an audience is living speech: spirit.

This image of spirit's fingerprint, beyond its mortifying associations, also argues that these worlds might touch, that there is some traffic between ephemeral speech and spirit and the grosser, disciplinary, and commodifying forms and forces of the administered world. Spirit, linked with the voice, leaves a very particular and even individual material trace, over and against enforced identities. And so while the camera and tape recorder might be responsible for the objectification of living spirit, it also seems necessary to note that, first, they register the existence of spirit—they testify that *there is* a spirit, something before and beyond the materiality of the recording, something anterior, something that might leave traces— fingerprints—behind in the material forms of its capture. In this sense, the tape recorder is a remembering of a living spirit, but a fragile one, and one too easily occluded by its reifying tendencies.

My wager here will be that Adorno's notion of immanent critique, a salutary corrective to some of the transcendent excesses of other theoretical modes, is most useful here: that the irreducible conflict between ideality and materiality that still might define the autonomous work of art might also, from another angle, be discerned in particular products of the Culture Industry. Adorno writes, "A successful work, according to immanent criticism, is not one which resolves objective contradictions in a spurious harmony, but one which expresses the idea of harmony negatively by embodying the contradictions, pure and uncompromised, in its innermost structure. Confronted with this kind of work, the verdict 'mere ideology' loses its meaning" (Adorno 1967a, 32). Immanent criticism depends for its efficacy on staying within the terms offered by its object; thus it does not and cannot proceed as a preformed method that can then be applied to a work, which would invite the charges of totalization and abstraction frequently leveled against theory and philosophy. Indeed, criticism's justice to its object, criticism's immanence, entails a revision of traditional scholarly methods and discourse. Writing of the essay, Adorno argues, "It wants to use concepts to pry open the aspects of its objects that cannot be accommodated by concepts, the aspect that reveals, through the contradictions in which concepts become entangled, that the net of their objectivity is merely subjective arrangement . . . [I]t constructs a complex of concepts interconnected in the same way it imagines them to be interconnected in the object" (Adorno 1991a, 23). This dense passage has far-reaching implications. First, the object, here our film, cannot be shoehorned into conceptual and propositional thought without leaving a remainder; and it is precisely that remainder, that aspect of the work of art that eludes and challenges the concept and that demands new concepts, that is of greatest interest. Second, that very remainder presents a welcome challenge to the concept, in unmasking its subjective foundation. And third, the particular elements of the work of art are to be considered as a complex, or (as Adorno, borrowing from Benjamin, writes elsewhere) a constellation, a nonhierarchical and contingent structuring of its immanent elements that can only be evoked and apprehended through thought's mimesis of that constellation. That is, criticism, thought, theory, and philosophy must evince a special affinity with the work of art; for Steven Helming, Adorno's immanent critique then names

"not only a critical program but also a performative one"—
that is, a dialectical one (Helming 2005, 98).

So a paranoid and violent film demands a paranoid and
violent thought, a thought that eschews the temptations and
the alibis of a suspect and sovereign objectivity. For just as the
material particulars of the work of art come to reveal their
truth content, so, too, must the conceptual abstractions of
thought be compelled to reveal the sublimated experiences
that prove to be their conditions of possibility. As Simon
Jarvis puts it, "[b]ecause . . . concepts always carry buried
within them, even when they look entirely abstract, the
traces of bodily pleasure and suffering, fear or desire, critically interpreting conceptual contradictions can be a way of
critically interpreting real social experience" (Jarvis 1998, 6).
For the theorist, concepts must come from the constellation
of material particulars; otherwise conceptual thought remains
beholden to its own repressed content. But aesthetic theory
and philosophy are impossible to the extent that they are
compelled to translate the nonconceptual truth of art into
a necessarily conceptual form—for example, while thought
can represent suffering, only art can express it. And it is this
delicate business of translation that risks the fingerprinting
of spirit.

Kiss Me Deadly seems to have little enough interest in the
concept, thought, or ideation at all. Its pleasures, first, seem
affective and sensory: the pleasures of the image and sound;
the pleasures of sex and speed; and the pleasure, finally, of
violence. But the violence in and of this film functions as
more than mere perverse spectacle. It becomes an index of
the depth and extent of conflict, contradictions social and
formal, material and conceptual, implacably pushed to their
limit—that is, violence here will fulsomely register the materiality of thought and the truth content of the material, with
the violence itself a testament to their irreducibility. The
film's violence works on bodies in the film but soon extends
to art and to thought, including, too, the wresting apart of
sound and image, such that the violence in the film will also
be a violence projected onto the film itself, as if even representation was too positive, the immaterial filmic image too

material. From this perspective the film's violence even registers, ambivalently, a violence directed toward thought but
also the violence of thought itself. Mike Hammer, the violent
materialist, rejects all thought, reflection, and art; but there is
also a violence here directed toward the violence of thought,
toward that thought that seeks to enforce specific identities
and ideologies, particularly over the women, a thought and
a thinking that aims at domination. Beholden to its own
immanence, this thought affirms that this is all there is—but
this is where that other violence erupts as an uncontainable
excess. This violence registers social conflicts to be sure, to
be found in both the film's form and content; but in its very
excess, this astonishing film becomes a well-nigh dialectical
engine of negativity, one that aims not at the suspect positivity of conceptual sublation but rather at the preservation of
the particular and the nonidentical, of the negative as negative, of art and thought as critical.

A cultural/materialist gloss of Aldrich's *Kiss Me Deadly*
might well start with a survey of its origins in the oeuvre of
Mickey Spillane. But if the novel can tell us much about its
particular context and mode of production—and do so in
unimpeachably materialist terms—its status as a historically
situated commodity also offers up an opportunity to think the
limits of the material. First, Spillane's particular form of textual production both extends and breaks with its most nota-
ble historical antecedent, the pulp magazine. While we might
want to consider the ways in which *pulp* as a term comes to
stand for all that modernism found abhorrent about popular
culture, for that grosser materiality from which a modernist
aesthetic sought to distinguish itself, we will first want to register how the pulps proved fertile sources for film noir during
the war years (as has been extensively documented by James
Naremore, among others[1]) but also how wartime shortages
did away with the pulps in short order. Spillane, with the
paperback edition of his first novel, *I, the Jury*, inaugurates
a decisive transformation of the mass cultural marketplace,
of pulp into paperback, virtually creating that category at a
stroke, as well as (not incidentally) demonstrating the extent
to which there remained a huge market for what had been the

pulps stock and trade: sex and violence, or, more properly, sex *as* violence, now suitably amplified to meet the desires of a traumatized postwar culture. Pulp here in this historical moment takes on a very slightly more tangible form: if pulp conjures up an unstable mess, neither solid nor liquid but properly abject, both in its material referent and also in terms of its perceived cultural value and attendant liberal *dégout*, the new form of the mass market paperback, still a commodity, testifies to a congealing, a becoming-material of a certain type of demonized text.

And yet famously, even ironically, Spillane ordered Signet Books to pulp fifty thousand copies of *Kiss Me, Deadly* because the publisher left the comma out of the title.[2] While it seems diverting enough to think of the man who wrote such prose as "Her breasts were precocious things" (*The Big Kill* 1951) obsessing over punctuation, there is a beguiling shift for us here, as what came from the pulps returns to pulp, as *pulp*'s signified shifts from plural noun—*the pulps*—to verb—*to pulp*. Pulp is pulped; having achieved a marginal materiality beyond its saturated and sodden beginnings, it returns to them again. What was approaching solidity melts into soup.[3]

I have raised this digression to serve a number of purposes: first, as a foregrounding of a waning of materiality at the level of the commodity itself—a waning that the film will itself come to thematize in a particular and fascinating manner; second, for its minimal trajectory, which again the film will adopt, as it reflects in an obsessive way on the passage from living flesh to abject corpse to resurrection; and third, to complicate the soupy materiality of pulp through the introduction of some air, a breath, whose first figure for us is that comma absent from the pulped lot of paperbacks—the comma that Aldrich and his screenwriter A. I. Bezzerides didn't deign to include in their film's title, either, earning them the wrath of Spillane, who one imagines, would have wanted to pulp the film prints, too.[4] The comma, according to the *OED*, derives from the Greek *komma*, meaning "something cut off, a short clause," its origin attributed to Aristophanes of Byzantium who deployed dots alongside a verse to indicate the number of breaths a speaker would need in recitation. Here *komma* refers to the verse itself, not yet the mark. But minimally the comma still retains its relation to the cut and to the breath. And if the comma is absent in Aldrich's title, we will find its work reappear again and again in the film, not in its grammatical guise, organizing and disambiguating text, but rather as a cutting and fragmenting—that is, formal and ideational—and a breathing, embodied and palpably material. The mark, or rather the work for which it stands, no longer regulates performance or textual production of meaning, or even finds an analog in the rhythm of the film's edits—what Metz called the filmic grammar and syntax—but works instead in the image and in the body, in the image of the body and the body of the image.

The comma marks the breath; the breath is the condition of possibility for the voice. The film begins with a breath—the breath *precedes* the image, just barely. Of all the inversions and subversions this film will enact, this one may well prove be the most crucial. The opening sequence emerges from the darkness insisting on a fragmentary and fragmenting logic, a refusal of a more classical Hollywood unity: as the score assails us, we witness a woman's naked legs, running down the highway. Christina (Cloris Leachman), who later will be tortured, her legs then as now betraying the shattering logic of the film, comes to be pinned like a specimen by the headlights of Mike Hammer's (Ralph Meeker) approaching car, her body a sign and cipher, an *X*, a cross. But the blackness from which she has emerged is also the blackness from which film noir and cinema itself emerge; and Hammer's car headlights, like another source of light (if not enlightenment) this film will offer, evokes the projector itself, as the title credits roll over the windscreen of the car through which—at which?—Hammer, Christina, and the audience look.

The image—or, better, the supposed integrity of the image and sound—is questioned before it is asserted, as these fragments assume an uncanny autonomy: neither the body nor the image can be thought of as a locus of identity, integrity, and presence; rather the image and body—and the woman's body in particular—seem pre-Imaginary, lacking gestalt, unsynthesized and unsynthesizable, their fragmentation anterior to any Imaginary integrity or Symbolic structure. This fragmentation is accompanied through the opening sequence and through the credits by Christina's panting breath, a breath pointedly embodied, indexing her exhaustion, the labor of those detachable legs. As the credits crawl in reverse across the screen, we cannot help but be struck at the terrible invasive intimacy of this panting. It is too loud; it is too close. It is also sexual, a point affirmed by her nudity under the trench coat. Christina's voice is signaled as a kind of excess—not one over and above the image precisely, but an excess related to the body—beyond language or sense, Christina's panting, thick with anxiety, exhaustion, and sex, seems the voice *of* the body, presubjective and somatic. In a manner analogous to the fragmentation of her body by the camera in this sequence, her sobbing breaths both assert and simultaneously question the link that ties voice and breath to body—it is patently *of* the body, yet curiously free of its bodily origin.[5] How can it be both? And against Christina's sobs the film juxtaposes Nat King Cole on the radio—both are excessive voices, embodied but in excess of the body, estranged from their origins and causes. But Cole's voice—the man's voice—only implies bodily support.[6] Why?

For Kaja Silverman, this gesture aligns the film with what she refers to as "talking cure" films—that is, the tendency or trope within classical Hollywood melodrama to externalize feminine interiority and consciousness. In Silverman's reading, women are represented as outside of themselves, particularly if we are too quick to map the self onto the body (Silverman 1988, 42–71). In contrast, Hammer's nemesis in the film, Dr. Soberin (Albert Dekker), derives his power from his status *as* voice, as he exists beyond the ability of the frame and the image to encompass him. The film demurs from showing him speaking or indeed from showing him at all: we see only his shoes while we hear his voice, as his power seems to derive from this uncanny and persistent separation of voice and body. For Michel Chion, Soberin is an exemplary *acousmêtre*: that is, a disembodied voice, a "form of 'phantom' character specific to the art of film" (Chion

1994, 128) that derives a significant mystery, omniscience, and omnipotence from its absence in image. We might also think of Hal from *2001* or the Wizard of Oz here, or even the narrator's voice in so many documentaries, a voice that is often referred to as the "voice of god." Of course it is only when the doctor's voice is put back in his body, synchronized with his image, that he can be killed: the voice's power over the soft and pulpy body, its own and others, demands an uncanny separation from its own material support, its bodily origin. But this separation, like Nat King Cole on the radio, is available only to men.[7]

The film violently asserts this power when Christina and Hammer are run off the road, and Christina's voice and body prompt further questions. The invisible doctor will demand the torture of Christina, making her body and voice an issue again, in both immanent and extrinsic senses. We cannot see her mouth, just her legs, flailing with pain; and the invisibility of her mouth, the source of the screams we hear, gives those screams, like her earlier panting, a curiously detached quality; they seem relatively disembodied for what is surely one of the ultimate experiences of embodiment—that is, torture, with a pair of pliers, no less. The criminals seek the location of what we will come to call the Great Whatsit, which will be the object of Hammer's quest—but they also seem to seek something else, acting as if it resided not in her psyche, but buried in her flesh. So they *dis*member her, taking her apart to get at her secret, a literalization of the figurative dismemberment of her body by the camera in the opening sequence and the antithesis of her injunction to Hammer, "Remember me." What are they looking for but the *source* of those screams, that voice? Her secret, the Great Whatsit, the body and the voice are then linked. It is as if they, too, recognize and enforce the gendered aspects of the *acousmêtre*, as they look for the voice in the body. So in Soberin's case, the independence of the masculine voice depends on its transcendence of the body, whereas this ambiguous quasi-independence of the feminine voice implies the body as such, the voice as embodied, the inability of woman to be an *acousmêtre*, pure and powerful voice.

Figure 2.1   Christina's legs

One the one hand, women's voices must be traced back to their source in the body; only masculine voices can be allowed the power of the *acousmêtre*. On the other hand, this penetration of the body of the woman, to divine her secret, what is in her more than herself, seems to imply a fleshly basis for subjectivity as such, revealed as suffering flesh. At what should be the revelation of the voice's origin and embodiment, a kind of hinge upon which psyche and soma turn, we find instead dead flesh, flesh that in its very suffering chastises us for the folly of thinking that we, like Descartes with the pineal gland, might locate the voice or ego or consciousness—or the soul—in the body. But more pointedly, perhaps, it also registers anxieties about anxiety: that is, anxiety is produced by and through an encounter with the real, an encounter with an object outside of symbolization. Christina's body is thus at once empty and full: empty of the secret her torturers seek, but also full of an impossible presence and meaning that resists language.

Christina's refrain in the film is "Remember me"—and yet the men here are more in the service of *dis*memberment and death. To put it slightly differently, just as her body is

taken apart under torture, Hammer himself is incapable of
re-membering, re-assembling the causal chain of clues and
evidence because of his own narcissism, his own fears about
bodily integrity—he is, as another character remarks, a "bedroom dick," not the detective in his classical guise as the subject supposed to know, but rather phallic and narcissistic. We
might have good reason for thinking that this is less mere
play than a critical take on the body as ground or origin.
Žižek puts it this way: "an unbridgeable gap separates forever
the human body from 'its' voice. The voice displays a spectral
autonomy, it never quite belongs to the body we see, so that
even when we see a living person talking, there is always a
minimum of ventriloquism at work: it is as if the speaker's
own voice hollows him out and in a sense speaks 'by itself,'
through him" (Žižek 2001, 58). The film, however, makes
this separation even more radical, as the voice comes to seem
an effect without a proper cause, and this despite the terrible,
invasive intimacy of the camera as well as the violence that
attends it. The body here is never just or quite the voice's origin, and thus we can only consider the voice in a paradoxical
way: both as embodied, indeed, as the secret or truth of the
body, but also as what is in the body more than itself, its
algalma, as Lacan would put it, the object-cause of desire, a
beautiful thing in a worthless or indifferent container.[8] Lacan
in another context invokes the French pun of *plus-de-corps*,
which might be helpful here: an excess *of* the body as well as
no more body, *in* excess of the body.

For Lacan these penetrations of the woman's body are doubly evocative, as he remarks in his gloss of Freud's famous
dream of Irma's injection, in which Freud looks in the mouth
of one of his patients who has not responded well to his
treatment and notices nasal bones growing in her throat:
"The first leads to the apparition of the terrifying anxiety-
provoking image, to this real Medusa's head, to the revelation
of this something which properly speaking is unnameable,
the back of the throat, the complex, unlocatable form, which
also makes it the primitive object *par excellence*, the abyss of
the feminine organ from which all life emerges, this gulf of
the mouth, in which everything is swallowed up, and no less

the image of death in which everything comes to its end" (Lacan 1988, 164). Fittingly, Lacan uses an image that the film itself will deploy: in the final sequence, Soberin identifies the Great Whatsit, the privileged object of everyone's desire here, as "The head of the Medusa"—something mortifying, a monstrously living part of an absent whole, explicitly feminine.[9] The penetration of Christina's body in the attempt to wrest her mystery from her, to find it through and in her suffering flesh, registers anxieties about life, too—its origins in the body of the mother—as well as death—here meat, mere flesh, the body emptied of its secret. One torturer asks Dr. Soberin if he should revive Christina, to which the doctor replies, "If you revive her, do you know what that would be? Resurrection, that's what it would be. And do you know what resurrection means? It means raise the dead. And just who do you think you are that you think you can raise the dead?" This Christ(ina) will not rise again.

But just as becoming an *acousmêtre* is gendered so, too, is resurrection, as Hammer, unlike Christina, survives this encounter to return, in the words of his buddy Nick, "Like Lazarus, back from the dead!" Hammer's resurrection is of an altogether more profane sort, as signaled by his phallic, violent name, which casts resurrection as erection. But we also register how this figure has risen again through our familiarity and even boredom with this recognizable or even exhausted type that rises again and again in genre film. The detective rises again because of, among other reasons, this figure's figuration of the processes of reading, watching, and consumption themselves—that is, its alignment with the viewer or reader, in interpreting material traces and clues to effect the production of meaning. The former constructs an absent narrative, while the latter consumes the one in process.[10] But *Kiss Me Deadly* presents us with a detective and a narrative that seemingly resist interpretation in that sense, and Hammer himself appears not only uninterested but also incapable of interpreting clues, the film's fragmented and aleatory narrative compounding this character's obdurate resistance to reflection. In this manner, *Kiss Me Deadly* begins to confirm what so many noirs knew all along: that masculine mastery of history and narrative has been up for grabs (if only figuratively) for some time, and this formerly privileged figure, the detective, whose power it seemed safe to assume, ended rather than began with Bogart as Spade or Marlowe.[11]

And this structural association of the detective figure with narrative also, here, effects a new relation to the voice. *Kiss Me Deadly*, whatever its conscious ties to the iconography and techniques of noir, cannot be said to deploy the voice in the same way as, say, *Double Indemnity* (1944), in which Walter Neff's narration into the office Dictaphone signals narrative closure in advance and at a stroke. In *Double Indemnity* it is not just the crime that has occurred in the narrative's past—as is the case in the classical detective narrative—but also its after-effects and consequences, not omitting the investigation and attribution of culpability and guilt, in this example worked through by Neff's superior Keyes.[12] Nothing of the sort is in *Kiss Me Deadly*, for which the uncanny and autonomous quality of the voice signals not an overdetermined narrative closure but rather the explosion of unities of all sorts, as we shall see. And in any event our interpretive guide here is shown to be wanting: distinct from the moral individualism of, say, Bogart's Marlowe or Spade—and lacking those figures' verbal skills—Hammer reveals himself as stupid, materialistic, and narcissistic. Within the generic terms of film noir this can certainly point to a decisive mutation or even exhaustion of a central category—that it is no longer possible or persuasive to present the detective as decisively powerful as Spade in *The Maltese Falcon* (1941)—but it may also be best considered for its formal function, for the way in which, along with the often dizzying and kaleidoscopic twists of the plot, interpretation of the brute events is no longer asked not only of the detective but of the audience as well—that the real mystery here is to be registered along another axis entirely.

If for Bogart's Spade or Marlowe all women are available and sex is a given, *Kiss Me Deadly* will surprise us, as every single time a woman makes herself sexually available to Hammer the act is not consummated—why? After he returns from the hospital, resurrected, we see him in a passionate clinch with Velda, but sex is deferred in favor of business. Hammer's brutal beating of a nameless thug follows the scene. He then tracks down Lily Carver, Christina's former roommate and figurative double, who like Christina is naked under a robe, visibly agitated and visually available. But Hammer doesn't succumb—there's a gun pointed at his crotch, suggesting how fraught sexual encounters are in this world and how they are linked to violence. And we see him with Friday, mobster Carl Evello's half-sister, who says, "Will you come into my house?" and whom Hammer will teach to say, "No." He is not the bedroom dick that the FBI labels him.

Hammer's "integrity" depends on a refusal of heterosexual relations in favor of masculine violence—his integrity is bodily, in distinction to Spade's ethical integrity. Even the kisses he and Friday exchange seem perfunctory and mannered, given with a camp brio that stresses their status as "liar's kisses," as Lily will later characterize them. Yet it is not enough to suggest that he sublimates heterosexual encounters in favor of masculine violence. When he arrives at the mansion of gangster Carl Evello, two thugs in the

Figure 2.2   Hammer, Sugar, and Charlie

cabana accost him. An extreme low angle shot from Hammer's feet withholds the substance of the encounter, leaving us only with an image of Hammer and Sugar's headless bodies meeting with an ambiguous but palpable *smack*, a meeting that leaves Sugar unconscious and the other gangster Charlie unsettled. "What did you do to him anyway?" Evello wants to know. "You scared Charlie half to death." Well, what did Hammer do? What has been withheld from us as viewers? What cannot be shown? What renders Sugar unconscious and Charlie afraid? It is a *kiss*—not a literal kiss, but not a liar's kiss either; not the mercenary kiss that Hammer deploys to keep his secretary Velda interested and onside, nor the perfunctory kiss he shares with Friday, nor yet the kiss that Lily will demand in the film's closing moments. It is an expression and consummation of desire that must be veiled by violence.[13] The wolfish grin on Hammer's face connotes more than the pleasure of meting out a mysterious and unseen violence—the pleasure of violence—but it also has to do with his encounter with brawny men in shorts in the cabana—that is, the violence of pleasure. It is also another index of the proximity of violence and desire in this world, and how the expression of the latter between men must be hidden by the former, more acceptable, mode of exchange. This kiss between the self-interested Hammer and the gangster tellingly named "Sugar" suggests even the masturbatory element that attends masculine narcissism, in which the Other, taken as an image of the self, becomes the ego-ideal with which the subject seeks erotic completion and fulfillment. Hammer wants to "kiss" someone just like Hammer: powerful, violent, morally compromised, criminal.

To put it slightly differently, Hammer's encounter with Sugar registers the fulsome ambivalence—that is, the mutual imbrication of narcissistic attraction and aggression—that characterizes the ego as an object of libidinal economy. Sugar is Hammer's reflection, his double, and so solicits his desire, but Sugar in his very status as double poses a threat to the ego's integrity as well as that of the body's imago—the same thing, Lacan tells us—which is only Imaginary and hence can be disassembled, fragmented, and so must be compulsively reasserted. In "On Narcissism," Freud writes, "The individual does actually carry on a twofold existence: one to serve his own purposes and the other as a link in a chain, which he serves against his will, or at least involuntarily. The individual himself regards sexuality as one of his own ends; whereas from another point of view he is an appendage to his germplasm, at whose disposal he puts his energies in return for a bonus of pleasure. He is the mortal vehicle of a (possibly) immortal substance—like the inheritor of an entailed property, who is only the temporary holder of an estate which survives him. The separation of the sexual instincts from the ego-instincts would simply reflect this twofold function of the individual" (Freud 1963, 78). Of interest here is less the agon of self-division that narcissism at once manages and exacerbates than Freud's pointed relation of narcissism to that element of the subject that seems immortal. The subject's conflict for Freud hinges on how from the narcissist's perspective sex tricks the narcissist, demoting him to merely "the mortal vehicle of a (possibly) immortal substance," alienating him from the body and its pleasure seen as its own property and undermining the ego. In this sense Hammer's displaced desire need not be thought of as solely a repression of bisexuality or homosexuality but also as linked via narcissism to a view of his body as property, even a commodity.

Unlike Spade, whom we considered in Chapter 1, who maintains his individuality at the cost of the repression of his desires, Hammer's narcissism and implication with commodities suggest a decisive shift, under which such narcissism testifies to the ego's fading, which necessitates its mimetic adaptation to the commodity form. That is, his repeated loss of consciousness is a kind of mimesis of the dead object, of death, as self-preservation becomes linked to self-destruction. In the context of the psychology of fascism—a descriptor generously applied to Hammer in critical literature—Adorno writes, "What takes place is that merger between id and superego that psycho-analytic theory already focused on, and it is precisely where the masses act instinctively that they have been preformed by censorship and enjoy the blessing of the powers that be" (Adorno 1967d, 80). The perversity of this principle can be registered on another level in the status of the Great Whatsit itself, as I shall go on to detail later.

Hammer's narcissism has been signaled in advance, if we remember his first line in the film—"You almost wrecked my car!"—to which Christina will later reply, "You're one of those self-indulgent males who only thinks about his clothes, his car, himself . . . Bet you do pushups every morning just to keep your belly hard." Hammer's bodily "hardness"—his bodily integrity, his ego—is maintained by commodities. But his endless stream of sports cars, "sweet rods," as Nick calls them, as well as what must be the first answering machine in LA, function to keep the masculine body intact, just as they inevitably undo the illusion of this integrity and self-sufficiency. A "sweet rod" means you're a man, but to be a man you need a "sweet rod," which can be wrecked, which you can lack. This succession of cars both denies and confirms castration as well as affirming masculine narcissism, and the answering machine returns us to the voice: like Echo in the myth of Narcissus, the voice on Hammer's machine is a woman's. This example of voice unhitched from the body seems banal or benign, but elsewhere it is figured otherwise. Masculine narcissism entails a specific structure of relations to the voice and image. If the image or double mirrors the narcissist, invoking a closed circuit of masculine self-enjoyment as in Hammer's encounter with Sugar, then the disembodied feminine voice potentially threatens that closed circuit—it is *another's* voice, and as such threatens to undermine the identity that the narcissist's gaze seeks to maintain. Unless they are only mechanically reproduced iterations, voices on tape, women's voices must be stopped at their source: the integrity of the masculine body as well as masculine identity as such is threatened by the (feminized) excess that is the voice. Encounters with the commodity, encounters with the double, and encounters with the feminine voice, even or especially when desired, threaten more than affirm the integrity of the masculine ego and must be met with violence. Indeed, we may, following Mladen Dolar's useful gloss, evoke the operative opposition inherent in the voice for psychoanalysis: "[T]he auto-affective voice of self-presence and self-mastery was constantly opposed by its reverse side, the intractable voice of the other, the voice one could not control. If we try to bring the two together, we could tentatively say that at the very core of narcissism lies an alien kernel which narcissistic satisfaction may well attempt to disguise, but which continually threatens to undermine it from the inside" (Dolar 2006, 41). These intimately and inevitably related characterizations of the voice perform two functions for us here: first, they precisely evoke the deployment of the voice in the film, in which women's bodies are probed and tortured to affirm the narcissistic integrity of the masculine ego, over and against the threatening excess that is the feminine voice; while the bodiless masculine voice standing for a deadly, even pathological agency itself cannot but also evoke the voice as an excess over and above the image and the body, a trajectory that ends in the psychotic experience of hearing voices, disavowed knowledge, and desires that return from the real. Or, to put it a bit differently, the arrest of the voice, Adorno's living spirit, technologically captured and reproduced, comes to speak to the instability of the arresting officer. Indeed, in its detailing how technology reifies the voice and spirit, the film comes to recognize its own implication in these processes.

For Hammer, resurrection can only be the compulsive spasms of phallic violence that eventfully occur to signal a desire that cannot be satisfied. Commodities and bodies are nominated as potential objects but finally only attest to the lack they were meant to fill; technologies meant to contain the spirit simultaneously suggest its reality. Yet over and against this widespread ambivalence of objects, the film notoriously provides an antidote in the form of a special and particular object that everyone desires, even as it terrifies some: the Great Whatsit, as Velda calls it. And the pursuit of this object coincides with yet another penetration of

Christina's body, an even deeper violation than her earlier torture that succeeds in grasping her secret where torture did not. Her autopsy yields a quite literal key to the place where the object of Hammer's quest—the Great Whatsit—will be found. This is a curious materialization, which I want to read this way: if the voice is that which is in us more than ourselves, if the voice is that thing of breath and body that is also the hinge of body and its secret—where the material meets the ineffable—can it be that here it is figured as a *literal* key that will open and reveal its origin and source? What will it show us?

The voice then, as well as being an index of gendered power, is also within the film's figurative economy *still too material* for what we are to be shown, and thus that secret point of its origin deep within the woman's body is transformed into another, more material figure, this literal key. The film dramatizes this excess of the voice in an analogously excessive sequence, one not drawn from Spillane's novel. No longer just the voice then, not the voice as an index of gendered power, not the voice as origin, as that thing that originates in the intimate depths of my body, that is at once mine

Figure 2.3   A deeper breath

yet also, always, extrinsic to me—the voice is underwritten by and stands in for something even less easily represented. Hammer confronts an elderly moving man who, sphinxlike, poses a riddle to the detective and the audience: "Makes you strong, a deeper breath. There's a house that I leave only once—I move in when I'm born and I move out when I die." For the mover the materiality of the body is rendered isomorphically with and as the trunk he carries: the body is a house and container, but also a load of consumer durables to be moved; the body is a burden, but it is also the house of breath, of spirit. Inverting Freud's pathologizing of the ego with the mortal subject as tenant to an immortal and material species-being, here the Italian mover's assertion of the identity of breath with spirit, the animating force of matter, is surely informed by a religious conception of the relationship between mind and body—the narcissist's tenancy is anxious, shallow, and pathological, a cause for worry over the body and its pleasures as property and even commodities, over the persistence of life beyond the individual ego; this one is deeper. "A deeper breath" evokes, potentially and variously, the incorporeal soul, vitalist essence, a universal animating energy, and some refined and rare interface between the mind and body. Indeed, *spirit* is derived from the Latin *spiritus*, which itself comes from the Hebrew *ruah* through the Greek *pneuma*—all these nudge us toward a construal of spirit here as vital, rather than spirit as psyche, which carries seemingly unwelcome (to this world) connotations of ego, subjectivity, and consciousness. "Move in, move out, always people come and go. One place they never leave, you know? 63 years I live in one place, the house of my body. Move in when I'm born, move out when I die," the mover adds, unconcerned with the fate of the body after the breath leaves it. And so a deeper breath is bound to the body only as it—temporarily—animates it. Elsewhere, the deaths of gangster Carl Evello and Hammer's friend Nick affirm this: Evello expires with a breathy sigh, punctured by a knife, while Nick's death is accompanied by the hiss of air from a car jack. "A deeper breath" is the breath that *precedes* the voice and psyche, that is their precondition, even less material and less mediated than voice, the flow of air over vocal cords, more originary, less substantial, ghostly—what Hegel might call *Geist*.

The mover's gloss on breath and spirit constitutes a call to remember that, whatever we are, we are not identical with our bodies, a call that reinflects all the other construals of memory the film has provided, particularly Christina's refrain (together with Hammer's profane "resurrection") and Soberin's interrogation of Hammer. Memory, here, in contexts both sacred and profane, must be nothing less than anamnesis, in both its Christian and classical guises. Thus Christina's injunction echoes Christ's from the Last Supper—"Do this in memory of me" (Luke 22:19)—while Soberin's question to Hammer—"What is it you are supposed to remember?"—ironically asks after an ideal knowledge, the knowledge of the soul or spirit driven out by the fall into the materiality of birth and the body.[14] In Plato's *Phaedo* the body and its senses come to be associated with error itself, requiring the purgation of catharsis so that a true remembering and thus knowledge might be gained. Yet these both inflect memory in differing tenses, as it were, with the first promising a resurrection and redemption to come (providing, of course, that we remember it is not yet), while the second demands we slough off the distortions of the body and its contingent material pleasures in an effort to attend the ideal, unchanging truth that precedes us and our fall into embodiment.

We might be tempted here to choose between these two types of memories and the consequences that trail in their wake. And yet the film will continue to exacerbate the contradictions between the two, playing off their conflicting implications, their pasts and futures. Nothing could be more toxic to materialisms of all stripes—not least that motivated by the detective figure—than religion as such, which comes to stand for the constriction of the mind to the dogma of the past. Moreover, these unlooked-for and even startling evocations of the sacred raise other questions: as something that is not supposed to exist anymore, especially here in an utterly commodified and wholly urban modernity, the reappearance of the sacred, together with a preponderance of religious iconography—sacrifice and resurrection, the soul and spirit—extend past a mere ironizing of the base materialism of this world. Fredric Jameson glosses this opposition in another context: "For the sacred can be supposed to have meant heterogeneity and multiplicity in the first place: a nonvalue, an excess, something irreducible to system or to thought, to identity, to the degree to which it not merely explodes itself, but its opposite number, positing the spaces for normal village living alongside the chthonic garbage heaps of the *im-monde* (Lefebvre) but also the empty spaces of waste and desert, the sterile voids that punctuates so many naturally expressive landscapes" (Jameson 1998, 22). And certainly it comes to function as such here, in its form as an irreducible excess—Christina's breath in excess of her body, the mover's "deeper breath," the various resurrections—and a nonvalue—here art and especially music, still minimally opposed to commodification and its systemic and enforced equivalences.

Soberin's Platonic call to remember requires further situating. In the source novel, the Great Whatsit, the object of Hammer's search, is heroin; if this has changed in the film, this is not to say that drugs are absent. Two instances are pertinent: Hammer's (not Irma's!) injection and gallery owner William Mist's self-administration of sleeping pills, which we will get to in a moment. Hammer, who has already been unconscious twice in the film, is captured and bound, spread-eagled and face down on a bed in a beach house, while Dr. Soberin injects him with sodium pentothal in an effort to find the location of the Great Whatsit. "What is it you must remember?" Hammer is asked, and when he flinches upon injection, the doctor adds, "Do not be alarmed, Mr. Hammer, it is only a harmless drug. Sodium pentothal . . . While you sleep your subconscious will provide the answer, and you will cry out what it is you must remember." Soberin poses as analyst: the narcotic dissolution of Hammer's intractable ego aims at a re-membering, a restructuring and reassembling of the truth of the subject via the unconscious. And Soberin poses as Platonist: the drug aims at liberating Hammer from the burden and error of his embodied existence so that he might remember the truth. But Hammer's depths, if such exist, are inaccessible to this particular *techne*, this analytic mode, and much of the remainder of the sequence is haunted by Hammer's wordless mumblings—the voice of the body rather than that of the unconscious or the ideal; a voice that finds a rhyme in the crash of the waves outside the beach house; or, as in Barthes, the voice as sheer grain, the voice beside or beyond language, meaning, and the ego.[15] His body on the bed is a figurative *X*, recalling Christina in the headlights and anticipating the fate of Evello.[16] But unlike Christina's body, Hammer's harbors no interiority, secrets, clues, or keys—only inchoate murmurs. And far from re-membering—intuiting the ideal before the body, or calling to mind repressed data and desires, but also assembling and integrating a phantasmatic body—here Hammer slips toward forgetfulness and oblivion.

And yet with the substitution of Evello's body for his own Hammer also plays on and with the voice, using misdirection and ventriloquism to trick Sugar into murdering Evello. Now the crash of the waves has been replaced by a radio broad-cast of a boxing match from the next room, emphasizing the conflict between these men. "Back among the living, huh?" Evello asks Hammer, while the sportscaster announces, "He has Bender up against the ropes now." It is Hammer who seems up against the ropes, tied as he is on the bed—but it is Hammer who is (a) "Bender," and it is Hammer who will rise again here profanely and sexually, as again his desire for the other, which is a desire for the same, must be medi-ated by violence. And as we cut to the next room, we hear Hammer imitating Evello: "Sugar. He talked. He's yours." Resurrection becomes erection, and Hammer's deceitful voice possesses Evello, promising another possession: "He's yours." The voice modulates from embodied inchoate mur-murings to something disembodied, something that feigns the possession of another body and that occasions not just further violence but the culmination of Hammer and Sugar's earlier kiss: Sugar sticks his knife in Evello (mistaking him for Hammer), and we are given Evello's dying breath in a rhyme with the escaping air of the car jack that crushed Nick earlier. Hammer kills Sugar offscreen—as with their previous encounter, sound, his screams, stands in for the act. But Evello's last breath, like Sugar's scream and unlike Christina's voice and panting, attests to little beyond thwarted and displaced desire. Here voices are thrown, projected, and dispossessed, dying breaths expelled—but there is in Hammer no overt recognition of the voice before or beyond the body, even as voices and breaths enter and exit the various bodies here on display. No balm for consciousness or unconscious alike, ambivalently tied to the body, drugs come to affirm a technology only nominally tied to truth. If Soberin uses drugs to get Hammer to remember his spirit before its embodiment, the effect instead is, again, the loosening of the voice and the breath from the body, with fatal consequences.

From here Hammer tracks William Mist, the art dealer cultivated by Velda. Velda has been given some names: "Carl Evello you know, but Dr. Soberin. Does that do anything for you? This joker [Mist] says there's new art in the world and this doctor's starting a collection." The doctor's association with art inflects the entanglement of matter and spirit in the context and fate of aesthetics in this profane world of commodities, masculine narcissism, violence, and torture. Earlier, Hammer, searching Christina's apartment, encountered orchestral music on the radio and poetry on her night table. Both are opaque to him, and ironically so, since it will prove to be the poetry of Christina's namesake—Rossetti—that leads him finally to the Great Whatsit: he is unable to associate the poem with her injunction to "Remember me." We should attend to this link between art and memory. Not only is art incomprehensible to him; he elsewhere actively destroys it, breaking a rare recording of Pagliacci while interrogating the tellingly unemployed opera singer Trivago, in another fraught confluence of voices and bodies.[17] But in this sequence, as a kind of motivation of the device, Mist's status as a dealer in contemporary art authorizes Hammer's crude break-in into the gallery and, more pointedly, his supreme indifference toward the art upon the walls and whatever memories they may stir. Indeed, this sequence may be seen as a summa of how *not* to look at art: uninterested in the particulars of the inarguably modernist paintings on display, Hammer, in his pursuit of Mist, passes all these individual works by—how could he do otherwise?—and what once might have been an engagement with a particular, even autonomous object, now relaxes into the merely aleatory, art as one thing after another. Threatened with discovery, Mist takes a handful of sleeping pills in order to escape Hammer's interrogation—sleeping pills prescribed by Soberin, again an agent of memory and forgetfulness, classical allusion and contemporary destruction, "sobering" reality and drugged reverie. And as Mist's consciousness seemingly escapes, we are, with Hammer, left with the brute fact of his imposing body, whose snores—again, too loud, in excess of their cause—irritate us and mock Hammer as much as modern painting, poetry, and opera have done.

Mist's very name emphasizes something of the liminalities with which the film plays—air and water combine to contrast ironically with his snoring, massy body. But it is also a sign: "Mist's Gallery of Modern Art" implies a well-nigh Hegelian trajectory for a modern art that has left behind architecture's "symbolic" materiality and the sculptural harmony of body and spirit in an attempt to realize spirit's trajectory, not as music, pace Hegel, but rather as immaterial and spectral "mist." Could it be that *modern art*, here immaterial and framed image, might not refer to painting at all but rather film? Art's difficulty or opacity, for Hammer and perhaps for us, seems linked to this abandonment of figuration and embodiment—in Hegelese, its tending toward spirit. But we might also discern a minimal Nietzschean aesthetic here: distinct from the classical clichés the sober Soberin offers, the drugged and snoring Mist, whose gross body ironizes his paintings' spiritualized abstractions, suggests a new gloss on the function of the Dionysian in "modern art" (or at least in this film's construal of the same). Art can no longer function as a truly Apollonian reconciliation of the individual to the tragedy of existence, or it can do so only in an inverted form, as it seems to in the case of Christina: the poetry of her namesake Rossetti and her injunction "Remember me" can no longer provide even a dream of reconciliation unless that is what death is—which is to say, much closer to the Dionysian death of self, though shorn of its collective and bodily pleasures. The masculine equivalent is to be located in Hammer's repeated loss of consciousness, in his drunkenness as he mourns the death of Nick (who is, significantly, Greek), and in his enforced abandonment of self under the influence of Soberin's injection. But the intoxicating supplement and its consequential dissolution of the self can never be marshaled to dissolve the stubborn lack that Nietzsche saw as constitutive of the individual's experience—the loss of self in intoxication carries no compensatory balm for lack in collectivity, as that prerogative has found itself usurped by the commodity form, to which liquor and drugs, the means, now owe their allegiance. Art, as it has functioned historically, founders here.

But Velda mentions that there is "new art" in this world, and Soberin is collecting it—or is he re-collecting it? For despite art's failure here, its insistent presence may suggest something else. Adorno writes, "The reality of artworks testifies to the possibility of the possible. The object of art's longing, the reality of what is not, is metamorphosed in art as remembrance. In remembrance what is qua what was combines with the non-existing because what was no longer is. Ever since Plato's doctrine of anamnesis the not-yet-existing has been dreamed of in remembrance, which alone concretizes utopia without betraying it to existence" (Adorno 1997, 132). Art squares the circle of anamnesis and resolves the opposition between the future tense of Christ's injunction and Plato's emphasis on the past, the overcoming of the body in the future and the present. If, in the diegesis of the film, art is irrelevant, incomprehensible, mere clue or *aide mémoire*, if art is here forgotten, it may be remembered; and in its memory it may evoke both an art and a world to come. Here the film remembers art, and not in the bad faith with which Hollywood typically addresses other media, including, enclosing, and trumping all older aesthetic forms—painting, music, dance, opera, literature, all encyclopedically evoked here in the film—in its self-presentation as a triumphant *Gesamtkunstwerk*, which this film works against in its pursuit of a more fragmentary form.[18] Nor is it just that the film seeks further to disparage its pulp origins, though that is certainly at stake, too, as it must realize its own implication in the commodity culture that Spillane's example has provided and of which Hollywood film is certainly a part—indeed, part of the film's fatalistic or even elegiac tone seems to stem from the supplanting of these older forms of art by the pulps and films. Rather, what Adorno's characterization of art might help us discern is the extent to which art, in its very being, even or especially at the moment of its passing away or irrelevance, materializes the ideal, the utopian—a future beyond bodily suffering that must be presented as a memory of the past before the body, a spirit that must remain merely ideal because of oppressive material constraints, and a utopia to come that cannot be represented within a world that would turn it into a commodity and a lie in the present.

Kiss Me Deadly then, finally, as art—implacably, impossibly seeking to negate what is in the memory of what might be. Dr. Soberin, art re-collector, finally collects the Great Whatsit, which will tell us what it means to evoke spirit in such a world, as well as what art is commensurate with it. Invoking the contrapuntal temporality of memory in art he asserts, "As the world becomes more primitive, its treasures become more fabulous." What does the key buried deep in Christina's flesh finally unlock and reveal? The key from Christina's body leads Hammer to the Hollywood Athletic Club to reveal another kind of excess secreted deep inside this place of bodies, bodies no longer particular and individualized like Christina's or the mover's but now collective and social, perhaps even narcissistic hard bodies and bellies like Hammer's, now generalized throughout the social sphere. What sort of spirit is secreted deep within this collective body—what then is the spirit of this age, its zeitgeist? In a locker in its depths is hidden the Great Whatsit.

This is the Great Whatsit, light that lives and the sound of breathing. If we review the itinerary I have tried to trace, from the sodden materiality of pulp, through inviolate, uncanny commodities and permeable, penetrated bodies,

Figure 2.4   The Great Whatsit

to voices shorn of material support, to the airy breath that precedes every utterance and evokes the spirit that stands behind it, we arrive here, at some kind of quintessence. Literally—but can we read this thing literally? Isn't it in excess of, at the limit of, the literal and material? Doesn't it precede the material (fiat lux!) even as it announces its end?—literally, it is meant to be some deadly fissionable radioactive substance, which returns us for a moment to the material determinants with which we began. For in the critical clichés that characterize film noir we also find anxiety about the atomic bomb, although the manner in which that anxiety finds figuration here is pretty much unprecedented. Charles Bitsch in *Cahiers du Cinéma* called *Kiss Me Deadly* the first film of the atom age,[19] and Godard borrowed from it for *Alphaville* (1965) and referenced it as late as *Notre Musique* (2004), just as this figure of the glowing box has been appropriated by such diverse directors as Spielberg in *Raiders of the Lost Ark* (1981), Alex Cox in *Repo Man* (1984), Quentin Tarantino in *Pulp Fiction* (1994), Luis Buñuel in *Belle de jour* (1967), and also David Lynch in *Mulholland Drive* (2001).

But if this is the beginning of a trope in film history, even motivated as a symbol, with varying degrees of success, it is also the end of something else. Its challenge to the nominal "realism" of the film (never strong to begin with), its challenge to logic and especially to the viewer, means that this object, this image, attempts to represent what is forbidden the image—its absurdity prompts Alain Silver, in a key essay on the film, to label it "pure phlogiston" (Silver 1996, 215), hypothetical, mythical, nonexistent. But better to put it in Adorno's terms, under which the Great Whatsit, from its name to its image and very being, assays the nonconceptual. Pure exception, at once concrete yet not identical with any attempt to render it knowable and sayable, it is beyond language and thought—but not art. It is the film's figure for itself, its own violence, and its own critical agenda, and it is the film's figure for film. The Great Whatsit, the head of the Medusa, comes to resemble nothing so much as the projector and camera themselves: a box, emitting light and sound, representing nothing itself, the condition of filmic representation that here implies and entails the end of all representation, ambivalently mortifying and animating. Not symbol, then, but allegory—not just or only the "invisible" pair of camera and projector, but the ultimate undoing and unfixing of the relationship between cinematic signifier and signified. At another moment in film history, a moment that is not this one nor our own any longer, theorists like André Bazin and Siegfried Kracauer described the goal of cinema as the redemption of the material world; but here there is little enough left to redeem (though not nothing, as I will suggest in a moment). The Great Whatsit and this film come to judge the world they have animated for us and do so by the very means by which that world has been animated, brought to life, spiritualized. Film, then, not as a disinterested or objective recorder of indexical traces, nor as the redeemer of material transience; but a film that has acknowledged its own role in the production of commodities, pulp culture, specific bodies, violence, its own being *as* a commodity. Not merely reflexive in a modernist sense, at the service of a particular authorial consciousness or aesthetic, here the apparatus is at once elevated and revealed; registering its place in this world it has brought to life and that it now consigns to flames. No critique, no critical vantage, is possible without this implacable and self-implicating box, ambivalently material and ideal, an uncanny animated and animating thing that brings life and death. This then is the film's deepest breath of all, or almost, as with its last breath it extrapolates the deadly logic of technology and material culture, of the masculine desire that ends in death and oblivion: to dematerialize this material, to blow it all away.

This, we might be forgiven for thinking, would be enough—the end of the film, the end of the world in an atomic fireball!—but we would miss then what in this world may be worthy of redemption. The ending begins with two kisses. Before she opens the Great Whatsit, Gabrielle solicits Hammer: "Kiss me, the liar's kiss that says 'I love you' but means something else. You're good at giving such kisses." And then she shoots him, before their lips meet. Hammer never has the chance to give another liar's kiss that speaks to a desire he doesn't really possess. But Lily kisses him with a bullet from her gun. This kiss, like all kisses, is like the voice and the breath, like the cut that is the comma—embodied, promising the explosive exchange of breath and fluid, it also implies the possibility of a less material exchange, of affect, desire, even love. Here, the kiss, in a context of displaced and repressed sexuality, impoverished language and commodity culture, cannot imply the circuit of Eros and Thanatos, as Eros has been decisively dismissed in this world, leaving the reign of Thanatos unchallenged. Just as Velda mocks Hammer earlier, "Stay away from the window—someone might blow you a kiss," now Hammer has received that deadly kiss, has been blown that kiss and gets blown away by it. This kiss begins without a body—their lips never meet— but is rather a kiss *blown*, transported by an explosion, a kiss that travels through the air as if on a breath, as if animated and spirited, a kiss of air and lead that bites the body, even though blown.[20] It is material and spiritual; it is the kiss that Hammer has been awaiting.

But Lily also has a kiss to receive, a dialectical complement to this one that she blows: this other kiss comes from
the Great Whatsit. Her fiery immolation seems, in contrast,
a real kiss, an experience of shattering bliss that leaves her
screaming like Christina under torture. And if Hammer's
kiss has always been the liar's kiss, this kiss is true—as she
herself is kissed by the lips and tongues of light emanating
from the Great Whatsit, the projector/camera, a light and
voice and breath that consume her. What might in another
register be called *jouissance*—a martyrdom of pleasure as we
witness the soul witnessing its own immolation—is here the
film's final *revelation* of the soul, a testament to its reality,
even materiality, at the moment of the consumption of the
body. The Great Whatsit, then, the Medusa's head, mortifies
the body only; if there is no redemption for Hammer or for
his world of violence and commodities, the Great Whatsit
deems that there might be redemption for Gabrielle. Gabrielle begins the film as Lily, Christina's double. This passage
from Lily to Gabrielle—from emblem of Easter and thus
the Resurrection to the angel, mediator between the human
and divine, who announces the end of (pre)history, the Last
Judgment, and the Second Coming—suggests that Gabrielle *is* Christina's Second Coming. Christina resurrected as
Gabrielle: though both women suffer bodily, their spirits
fingerprinted, Gabrielle, embodied and enflamed, is transported bodily, and therefore Christina is, too. Departure and
parousia coincide. She is risen; she is remembered.

Or, put otherwise, the film, so fixated on the permeability
and fragility of the body, its wounding by violence and gun-
play, its opening up under torture and autopsy, its penetration in and in violence, and its delusional and masculine
implication in narcissism, has shown us bodies *beside themselves.* No longer mere matter or mass or meat, no longer self-
contained or simple enclosure, no longer then a darkness—a
mouth, a womb—the body is yet a mystery and a question,
one that points to itself—what am I in myself?—and points
beyond itself—what is in me more than myself? This mystery
is certainly what leads Jean-Luc Nancy to argue, "The signi-
fying body—the whole corpus of philosophical, theological,

psychoanalytic, and semiological bodies—*incarnates* one thing only: the absolute contradiction of not being able to be a *body* without being the body *of a spirit*, which disembodies it" (Nancy 2008a, 69). Where Gabrielle's immolation departs from Christina's torture and autopsy is in its implication of body and spirit: as the radioactive flames—and her screams—rise, her body can no longer be thought of as a house for spirit, the container of a breath and a secret, like the mover's trunk or indeed the Great Whatsit itself. And dialectically, the spirit is therefore no longer just a breath, a secret, a voice, a homunculus, a less material double of the body it "inhabits" and from which it seems to emerge. The breath or voice or spirit that passes from orifice, bullet holes, incisions, and wounds is thus no longer a metaphysical or ideal entity but rather a testimony and testament to the body itself, to the body as that which suffers. The suffering of the body renders it most itself and simultaneously beside itself, in excess of itself. Suffering shifts and transforms the pair of spirit and body; suffering means, for example, the end of "the" body, an idealized and abstract singularity that stands in for an incalculable multiplicity of bodies. And so suffering here means the end of the spiritualization of "the" body, even the spirit of the body. What we are left with then, what the film has prepared for us and us for, is the body of the spirit, even the spirit made flesh. Gabrielle on fire, sacrificed not to her "feminine" curiosity, disparaged by Soberin in terms of Lot's wife and Pandora, is the real figure of death but especially of resurrection and the truth of Christina's resurrection: not Hammer's profane erection, nor even Christ and a sacrifice to the Father to reaffirm that Father, but instead a woman's sacrifice. In a spirit that echoes the film's dominant tendency of inversion from the opening credits and after, far from being a punishment of the femme fatale for her desires, this conflagration can only be redemption. The femme fatale's "transgressive" sexuality, her scandalously improper appetite for power, and even her insatiable curiosity are not to be seen as punished by a masculinity sublimated in and as a nuclear weapon. If she had been a vamp or a witch, her immolation here might also be affirmed historically, by a precursor drawn not from the rich iconography of noir that the film so knowingly exploits but rather from another context entirely: Dreyer's *The Passion of Joan of Arc* (1928).

The comparison is instructive. For many, Dreyer's film structures itself around an interpretive aporia: Joan's authenticity, her expressiveness, is guaranteed by the camera's devotion to her suffering face, which is given to us only on the condition that we refrain from identifying with this character. In contrast, the film's implacable fragmentation of space into highly stylized surfaces at once guarantees Joan's authenticity and morality at the same time it undermines— even deconstructs—the narrative, alerting the viewer to the extent that the film demands an allegorical reading to reconcile stylistic conflict with thematic and narrative coherence.[21] While *Kiss Me Deadly*, unlike Dreyer's film, has expressed no equivalent devotion to Lily/Gabrielle's face—or, pointedly, to the humanist values that entail such devotion—it has instead stressed the identity of Christina and Lily/Gabrielle in figurative and structural terms and done so over and above the merely ethical characterization of the former as "good" and the latter "bad": both have short blonde hair, both are introduced naked under a coat or robe, and the film begins with Christina and ends with Gabrielle. That is, it has asserted their identity in mimetic and aesthetic rather than essential terms, even as both films affirm and indict women's suffering. If Dreyer succeeds in rendering the divine human and material, even embodied, Aldrich succeeds in suggesting the material may be transcendent.[22] But where is there to go? Just as there can be no privileged perspective in this world, the camera's or a character's, so, too, there can be no image of what might lie outside this world—what is beyond the suffering of the woman's body, beyond all bodies, beyond commodities and technologies, beyond breath and voice, beyond the beach house and the relentless waves that ceaselessly mark this final location as a verge and a limit, can only be implied and never shown. Gabrielle's transport as a suffering body must not and cannot be represented without lapsing into ideology.

And as for the woman, so for the film: what seems nihilistic, an indictment of all that is, distinguishes itself from nihilism by this mimesis of nihilism, the assumption of a perspective marginally removed from what is—an audacious perspective of redemption, all the more audacious coming from a commodity film and a film obsessed with commodities. To be sure, this is not to offer, contra Marx, a metaphysical explanation for the materiality of suffering, reification, and the uncanny allure of commodities or how they speak to and through the ego, as that sort of metaphysics seems always a sign of mystification or at least error. Alternatively, this is itself a kind of anamnesis: a remembering of what materialist thought depends on. Here instrumental thought—masculine violence and its attendant commodities and technologies—cannot do without myth and superstition even as it continually seeks to suppress them: woman as excess, Pandora, Lot's wife, the femme fatale, fetishized commodities, voices as ghostly, boxes as magical, and the fabulous treasures of a world at once modern and primitive. And similarly, this world's dogmatic insistence that this is all that there is, an ideology of consumption, overdetermined gender roles, containment of both body and narrative, and delimited and fragmented space all express a captivity to its own immanence—this is itself a suspiciously transcendent claim, legislating as it does that the future can only resemble the present and the past. That is, even this sheerly negative representation must also entail metaphysics, as all thought of the material—and especially critical thought—depends on an impossible, excessive thought from the outside, even as thought's desperate bid for such a transcendent vantage in no ways secures that perspective. Anamnesis, finally, names the irreducibility of materialism and metaphysics to each other. What thinkers of both cultural and theoretical drifts must remember is the commensurability between a thought of the material and the materiality of thought. The name for such a commensurability is the dialectic.

Kiss Me Deadly gives us a world wholly as "indigent and distorted" as Adorno could ask; and though the light it shines on that world fixes it and objectifies it in a manner much more profane than sacred, that light also negates it and undoes it. Transcendence appears as immolation; this is the only way it can be represented—that is, negatively—from our point of view, from within this corrupt world and our own. Lily is kissed by the light and fire of Great Whatsit, whose kiss affirms Lily's soul as body and body as soul. She leaves the beach house where this scene is set, in screams, in a transport, on a deeper breath.

CHAPTER 3

NEGATIVE DIORETIX

REPO MAN (1984)

Every work of art is an uncommitted crime.
　　　　　　　　—Theodor Adorno *Minima Moralia*

DEBBIE　Come on Duke, let's go do those crimes!
DUKE　　Yeah, let's go get sushi and not pay!
　　　　　　　　　　　　　　　　　　—*Repo Man*

If, as I have tried to suggest, both *The Maltese Falcon* and *Kiss Me Deadly* attempt an impossible reconciliation of their status as commodities with their ambitions as art, here, unpromisingly enough, in *Repo Man* we come to be confronted with virtually everything we might have thought stood opposed to the sort of Adornoian aesthetics I have traced. For example, can a comedy evince the kind of seriousness that Adorno values in art? Can a work that so insistently foregrounds its assemblage out of the most formulaic and discredited genres come to embody the singularity and particularity Adorno insists upon as constitutive of the work of art? The film bombards us with a virtual litany of such genres and cultural modes: punk rock, Blaxploitation, the spaghetti Western, science fiction, road movie, teen comedy, the conspiracy thriller, sheer kitsch, and more besides. Yet, tempting as it might once have been, this is not the place to historicize this anthology of pastiched cultural detritus under the rubric of postmodernism, a concept and a problematic that itself, ironically, seems to have joined these genres in the trashcan of history.[1] Rather, it is here along the axis of genre (though not solely here, as I will go on to show) that the film asserts not an opposition (as in Jameson) to the illusory sheen of commodity-image nor merely an affinity to formerly abused cultural styles and modes—an ironic "negation of the negation" of what was distinctive about the modernist artifact—but a well-nigh ecstatic surrender to undifferentiated trash, the aim of which is to sift and identify—differentiate and particularize—some of the constitutive elements of what otherwise we can only conceive of as sheer homogeneity: trash.

From the vantage that *Repo Man* will provide, then, the lessons the uncanny objects—the Maltese Falcon, the Great Whatsit—will have had for us derive from their scandalous being itself, their residual singularity fleetingly though undeniably present as if to announce the passage of singularity as such; and more precisely, with the eclipse of even these notional masterpieces, we might discern the unfurling of a cultural field in which they cannot take their places as part of some absent but still-desired canon. Instead they persist as a kind of after-image within the great deterritorialized and de-differentiated field of culture as such, which will now come to signal little more but nothing less than the triumph of commodification and the imprint of sheer exchange value across the visual. From the residually modernist perspective that spectrally inheres in these earlier uncanny objects, what comes after is and can only be junk, immersive and cumulative—which must itself, then, become the new organizing frame, the ironic *terroir* within which to pose the question of the fate and function of art, or to ask if such a question can have meaning any longer.

Art, becoming junk, argues at once for both the obsolescence of an ideal and the persistence of that ideal, if in the almost unrecognizable form of trash. Might it even be that art, like philosophy in the polemic that opens *Negative Dialectics*, lives on because the moment to realize it was missed, and it persists not as a ghost or spirit, but rather now as simply trash? Capital and commodification having accomplished what philosophy and spirit could not, the end of art appears as a *fait accompli*—here, not the transition from the idealities of Romanticism to the transaesthetic vocation of modernism (as in Jameson's history of the passage from the beautiful to the sublime and finally to theory itself[2]), but rather an utterly material cancellation of what was to have been beyond mere use and exchange value, now as trash useless and indifferent to exchange. But wasn't this an end to which modernist art aspired, a modality that celebrated sheer uselessness and frustrated exchange, all the better to rebuke, implicitly or explicitly, the dominance of identity, exchange, and the commodity form? Could it be then that in some counterintuitive sense art's becoming junk coincides with the fulfillment of part of its critical ends? And if we may entertain this possibility for art, might it also be possible to see the same logic at work in relation to the fate of another junked and old-fashioned concept, subjectivity itself? "The death of the subject," whatever else it has come to mean from Foucault to posthumanism, testifies to a desire to pass beyond the torturous material and psychic opposition of subject and object, consigning it to the same fate as art. And while we're at it, why not theory, too, the very discourses that once sought to critique the subject and portend its overcoming under a bewildering variety of rubrics? Hasn't theory and especially film theory come to seem outmoded, sporting a mullet, dad in a Twisted Sister T-shirt passed out at the party? Haven't the multiplicity of modes of thought once offered as "theory" been largely reduced to junk in a discipline now under the spell of material history and material culture, as if those materialities were given and legible, preferences and alternatives to no-longer-fashionable modes of analysis? It might then be worth asking after the extent to which subjectivity and theory—like art—live on past their best before date, and more, come after their end to their paradoxical realization, a realization and fulfillment that can only occur after they are trash and trashed—indeed *because* they are trashed.

Here I will argue that *Repo Man* attempts nothing less than the repossession of "man," or better, a notion or sense of subjectivity, to be reclaimed or recycled from its fate as an ideological abstraction, a point of consumption, or, alternatively, the subject of domination. It does so by enacting a mimesis of trash, but a mimesis that is structured so as to reject what Adorno describes as the subjective domination of the object. Mimesis—again, not to be thought of as solely an aesthetic category—entails a radical openness to the object, a willful abdication of the impulse toward mastery and domination that elsewhere inheres in the subject's stance toward the object world, a stance that is revealed as the motor of *Dialectic of Enlightenment*. This mimetic strategy is affirmed, paradoxically enough, through the film's savage satire of Scientology, which it casts as *Dioretix: The Science of Matter over Mind*; but beyond its critical stance toward this bogus science and faith, beyond its savaging of institutions and structures of belief and exchange of all kinds, it comes to explore how subjectivity might be conceived through a surrendering of its will to power over the object and instead evoke nonalienated subjects and objects. Moreover, the film can do so only under the proviso that all the terms within this constellation—film, subject, and object alike—appear as trash.

Trash litters Adorno's writings, though not always where one might think to look—in his considerations of the Culture Industry and kitsch, for example, though it is there as well. In *Negative Dialectics*, he references Brecht approvingly: "[culture] abhors stench because it stinks—because, as Brecht put it in a magnificent line, its mansion is built on dogshit . . . All post-Auschwitz culture, including its urgent critique, is garbage . . . Whoever pleads for the maintenance of this radically culpable and shabby culture becomes its accomplice, while the man who says no to culture is directly furthering the barbarism which our culture showed itself to be" (Adorno 1973, 366–67). What must surely strike us in this passage is the extent to which here as elsewhere Adorno cannot but include his own position as entangled within the system he wishes to critique.[3] Defying his caricature as a mandarin elitist, Adorno fully implicates himself as a cultural critic, casting his agenda as garbage, his object as mired in dog shit—and yet, for all that, a rejection of critique or indeed of culture itself cannot be an option. He seems less Lukács's tenant of the Grand Hotel Abyss than a homeless man pushing a burdened shopping cart (though perhaps auditioning a cassette of Beethoven on a salvaged Walkman, in the absence of a Celan book on tape).[4] Is it despite or because of its shabbiness (leaving aside for a moment its culpability) that culture must be affirmed? As Robert Hullot-Kentor writes, "[i]n the *Dialectic of Enlightenment*, the Culture Industry that this country produced is 'barbarism.' This American 'barbarism is not the result of cultural lag,' as other European visitors to America speculated, he writes, but of progress itself" (Hullot-Kentor 2011). This is to say that culture is utterly implicated in and as barbarism and so earns all the opprobrium the critic might muster. This, too, constitutes the bad faith of the work of art—its own shame at its culpability, at its blindness and exclusions. Culture, which was to have been part of the process and progress of the Enlightenment, stands accused as sheer regress, and it is this precisely that must be affirmed and unmasked.

If what was thought to have value now stands revealed as worse than worthless, what then of the formerly worthless? What is the dialectic appropriate to trash? Could we think an aesthetics or philosophy of trash? As a noumenon, trash is *trash*: worthless, discarded, undifferentiated, indivisible, already presumably sorted, mined for recyclables and deposit bottles, for fodder for the Antiques Roadshow or eBay, or for Craigslist and garage sales. In this sense trash remains what Žižek calls the indivisible remainder, that which subsists after the exchange, after the unfolding of the dialectic, after foreclosure, beyond use and exchange values, in the space between desire and its object—trash is *Real* (Žižek 1996, 1–10). Trash earns its noumenal status by virtue of its existence at the periphery of symbolization and thought, the extent to which though ubiquitous we remain largely indifferent to it; and it even merits consideration as Adorno's nonidentical for lying defiantly outside of economies of language, culture, and thought. Indeed, could the ultimate paradox of trash inhere in its being simultaneously undifferentiated and irreducible? But as self-contained as it might seem, trash troubles any neat subject-object division, much as art has tried to do in the examples we have already considered: both art and commodification seek to make the thing speak, to turn the object into a subject. Thus the Maltese Falcon, sphinxlike, murmurs riddles of the familial resemblance of commodity and art, while the Great Whatsit seeks in an apocalyptic fire to legislate against the terms of the debate and to consign art and commodity both to the dustbin of history. Trash affirms not the object speaking but the subject spoken: the extent to which reification molds us, how we as subjects have become objects to ourselves, the consumer consumed. Yet outside my office window I can see in the mud a collective montage of Coke cans, cigarette butts, and paper, mingling with a cadence indifferent to the tempo of production and consumption, resolving fitfully into something other than the instrumental unity that characterized their lives as commodities, articulating an order wherein each piece of garbage might speak its particular history. As Julian Stallabrass suggests, "such an order, better than that of immaterial cyberspace, may serve as an image of an otherwise unrepresentable global capital" (Stallabrass 1996, 183).[5]

Adorno's reflections on trash are best approached by way of Marx and Benjamin. Most trash is the direct product of products, which is to say that it is the product of the consumption of commodities—as Marx says in the *Grundrisse*, "a product becomes a product only by being consumed. For example, a garment becomes a garment only in the act of being worn; a house where no one lives is in fact not a real house; thus the product, unlike a mere natural object, *becomes* a product only through consumption. Only by decomposing the product does consumption give the product the finishing touch" (Marx and Engels 1978, 91; qtd. in Stallabrass 2008, 172). Trash is not composed solely of the commodities themselves but also of their seductive packages that grant their specious status as subjects, inciting our lust, imparting in them a fetishistic power. "Decomposing" Marx says: as an intrinsic and constitutive element of the commodity, this decomposition argues that the commodity is inherently trash, as trash is the badly repressed truth of the commodity, what distinguishes exchange value from use value, or culture from nature.

Walter Benjamin's *Arcades Project* attempts to write the history of its present from the trash of the past, a history that is both cultural and philosophical, that eschews the grand narratives of another historical mode for a narrative that goes, as it were, against that particular grain, looking for and finding instead a history that is consciously produced and lived, and not the dream or spell of ideology. Benjamin begins with plans and notes and drafts around 1927 but never finishes this work before his suicide in 1940. It runs to over a thousand pages in its English translation. Captivated with how the Paris arcades of the nineteenth century enclose the streets—but particularly the shops—under glass, thus blurring the boundary between inside and outside, public and private space, Benjamin seeks an entrance to the mystery of commodity fetishism. Modernity depends on and is brought about by the commodity, which Benjamin sees as beginning to bloom and thrive in this new hothouse environment. For Benjamin the commodity form and architectural technology are concrete and material harbingers, to be read allegorically as past witnesses of the present. He describes his approach in these terms: "Method of this project: literary montage. I needn't *say* anything. Merely show. I shall appropriate no ingenious formulations, purloin no valuables. But the rags, the refuse—these I will not describe but put on display" (Benjamin 1999, 860). Despite this self-injunction to silence the text is more than a shop window displaying junk, as Benjamin does indeed say a lot himself, reflecting upon posters, the ornamentation of buildings, fashion, buses, cafes, Baudelaire and photography, as well as many other things, trashy and otherwise; but for the most part *The Arcades Project* remains a palimpsest of quotations. Approaching it for the first time a reader must surely submit in agreement to Benjamin's description and rummage through this bewildering and recondite "literary montage" with all the gusto of a credit-card-wielding shopaholic turned loose in a big box store or else be lost among the teetering piles of stuff. But the materials here deployed to evoke the modern moment, let us not forget, are not shiny and new, like that drum of ketchup at Costco, but "the rags, the refuse"—what a culture throws away. Benjamin's rags offer a necessary dialectical coda to Marx's description of the transformation of linen into coat in *Capital*, as here we are called upon to witness, over and over, the commodity's deliquescence.

Benjamin derives this approach from the surrealists, whose fascination with junk, with the outmoded commodity drained of all use value, fluoresces in aesthetic modes like collage, wherein the detritus of modern life finds a form that mimes the fragmentation and depthlessness of modern life, opposing the utilitarian values and smug instrumental rationality of the bourgeoisie.[6] Indeed, surrealism and especially collage promise beyond their critical function for Benjamin nothing less than an alternative form of rationality, a nonhierarchical juxtaposition of fragments that allows truth to emerge—in surrealism Benjamin finds crucial aesthetic counterparts to his constellational mode of thought, in that it proposes an immersion in the particular and material details of modern life, an immersion that eschews the abstractions of conceptual thought on the one hand and the aestheticist separation of art and life on the other.[7] Ultimately Benjamin finds the surrealist privileging of dreams to provide a means by which collective and utopian desires might be discerned amid the inauthenticities of ideology and commodification.

Aspects of Benjamin's investments in objects, surreal and otherwise, surely informed Adorno's thought, as well as his tribute to his friend. Of Benjamin Adorno writes, "He is driven not merely to awaken congealed life in petrified objects—as in allegory—but also to scrutinize living things so that they present themselves as being ancient, 'urhistorical' and abruptly release their significance. Philosophy appropriates the fetishization of commodities for itself: everything must metamorphose into a thing in order to break the catastrophic spell of things" (Adorno 1967c, 233). Just as in *Negative Dialectics* where Adorno wants "to use the strength of the subject to break through the fallacy of constitutive subjectivity" (1973, xx), here philosophy—theory, *critical* theory—must abandon abstraction and itself become a thing, even a fetish, an object of desire. To become a thing

to break the catastrophic spell of things—to surrender an
agency that we would habitually associate with the subject,
to model thought after what Sartre characterized as the *en-
soi*, the in itself, and mime a stone—what can this mean?
In a key film the situationists asked *Can the Dialectic Break
Bricks?* (René Viénet 1973). Is this a case of bricks breaking
the dialectic, obdurate materiality finally triumphing over
thought? This particular situationist *détournement* offers a
clue: Viénet appropriates a martial arts film and rewrites its
Manichean generic conflict as class conflict, in turn transforming a commodity into a critique. To put it another way,
it makes the trashy commodity speak to a better dream than
the one that constituted its manifest content.

But if this is how a committed art sought to become a
thing to critique the thing, what about thought? Indeed,
for Adorno, surrealist collage—and Benjamin's valuation of that form—seems always to stop short. It would
be useful here to contrast Adorno paying public tribute
to his great friend with Adorno at his more intimate and
critical. In a famous letter from 1938, Adorno argues that
Benjamin's literary montage, his ruin of rags and refuse,
desperately needs mediation, a concept crucial to both
thinkers and derived, like reification, from Georg Lukács.[8]
There are no social facts, final and complete in themselves, Lukács argues, as the seeming immediacy of these
facts is not only ideological but also always trumped by a
reality in the process of becoming—that is, social totality
mediates the alleged immanence of particular social facts.
Lukács describes this process as an attempt "to out-Hegel
Hegel"—a challenge if ever there was—by making the proletariat both the subject and object of history, thus making
freedom an objective reality produced by humanity itself.
Adorno continues: "The 'mediation' which I miss and find
obscured by materialistic-historiographical evocation, is
simply the theory which your study has omitted. But the
omission of theory affects the empirical material itself. On
the one hand, this omission lends the material a deceptively
epic character, and on the other it deprives the phenomena, which are experienced merely subjectively, of their real

historico-philosophical weight . . . If one wanted to put it rather drastically, one could say that your study is located at the crossroads of magic and positivism. This spot is bewitched. Only theory could break this spell" (Adorno and Benjamin 1999, 283). Benjamin's is not yet then a thought that adequately mimes the object; and the signal terms evoked by Adorno—*empirical* and *magic*, both only ever raised to be critiqued—take pains to stress how the object is not and cannot be thought to be immediately given, and how for him, Benjamin's thought threatens to relax into the merely affirmative. For Adorno surrealism and particularly collage entail an abdication of subjectivity in favor of chance and a concomitant refusal to mediate the component elements, resulting in a fetishization of reified immediacy, what Benjamin himself would call homogenized, empty time. Here we can read a version of the charge he has leveled at Benjamin, whose method, to put it in slightly different terms, is less montage than collage—which is to say, less dialectical, since it is *theory*—or more precisely, theory's *absence*—that conjures this bewitched spot, where things, commodities, appear to speak for themselves.

Yet among these rags of Benjamin's also moves a figure capable of providing a mediatory role. Adorno continues, "I am referring to the 'ragpicker.' It seems to me that his role as the figure of the lower limits of poverty is hardly captured by the way in which the evocative term is actually used in your study . . . I wonder if I am actually exaggerating in assuming that your failure to do so is related to the fact that the capitalist function of the ragpicker—namely, to subject even rubbish to exchange value—is not articulated" (Adorno and Benjamin 1999, 284). But we have just characterized the *Arcades Project* as a history of rags and refuse, and we should now also pause briefly to characterize Benjamin himself in this context: Benjamin, whose letters to Adorno also include litanies of trouble, migraines, and grinding poverty and who sifts through the libraries of Paris like a ragpicker, filling notebook upon notebook with the bright tatters of forgotten objects and forsaken history. Does Adorno suggest a barely hidden identity between Benjamin and the ragpicker, one that his friend seems neither to recognize nor repress? Or rather is Benjamin circumspect about subjecting "even rubbish to exchange-value," albeit in a philosophical register? Speculation raises a paradox: is the ragpicker finally a rag, too, forsaken and discarded, just another thing on display, unfulfilled or spent potential? How can we know the ragpicker from the rags?

Following Lukács, for Adorno reification determines social relations between things and objective relations between people. This cannot merely be shown but must be tirelessly demonstrated, by means of revealing and stressing the mutual imbrication of material-empirical understandings and interpretive-hermeneutic ones. For Adorno, if Benjamin's project properly—but ultimately only ambivalently—grants priority to the object, it misses the opportunity to reflect further on how those objects mediate not only each other but the subject, too. It misses the opportunity to think and theorize the ragpicker, who stands in a complicated relation to both subject and object: a person become both a thing and a subject that mimes its object and so enables the potential redemption of subject and object both. More, it becomes tempting to read this figure of the ragpicker as allegorical not just for Benjamin but for the materialist philosopher, theorist, and historian who strays too far into empiricism and positivism, echoing Husserl's cry that initiates phenomenology—"To the things themselves!"—but losing along the way the extent to which things, objects, and even ideas are not and cannot be immanent in that sense. To be a ragpicker, then, entails being a rag while being more than a rag—it entails mimesis but also discrimination, interpretation, and theory.

Trash, rags, ruins, things, and objects—if we are to think of the ragpicker and the rags as suggesting new possibilities for the relation of subject and object, we must further clarify what it means to be an object. Object is from the Latin *objectum*, "something thrown before, or over against." In its very origins, the object is defined implicitly against its other, the subject—which is to say, in the very act of definition it is dominated by the subject, who magisterially sets the terms under which the object will be grasped. For Kant in the *Critique of Pure Reason* the "Object is that in the concept of which the manifold of given intuition is combined" (B137), rendering the object as object of experience and of consciousness. Broadly speaking, Kant draws no distinction between a real object and an object of consciousness, knowledge, and action. In *The Science of Logic*, Hegel extends Kant in two ways. First, the particularity of the object must stand over and against the independent concept—that is, the subject is "the manifold world in its immediate existence" (§ 1536) the particular, which the concept or the I must overcome on the way to knowledge, preferably of the absolute variety. But second, the object is closer to "the in and for itself, which is free of restriction and opposition"—that is, *from* a subject. The subject must then *submit* to the object, rather than overcome it; and it is precisely here that we find a thread Adorno will take up in his thought. But Hegel extends these views, too, distinguishing further between *Objekt* and *Gegenstände*, with this latter to be understood to suggest something more like an obstacle. In his *Encyclopaedia of Philosophical Sciences*, Hegel characterizes the *Objekt* as the correlative of the subject, being an object *of* something or someone, thus implicating the object in a web whose complexities mirror the subject's conceptual activities of judgment and inference. But the *Gegenstände* is an intentional object, an object of knowledge, and so in a sense already contained and determined, not least by our senses and psyches. Abstracting particular qualities that we conceptually ascribed to a *Gegenstände* leaves us with an abstract *Objekt*. However, this act of abstraction, the sublation of subject and object that for Hegel is part of the dialectic, leaves a remainder, some rags, not unlike a Starbucks cup after I've sublated my usual—a grande cappuccino—in my own version of trying to get the subject—me—and object— here, steaming coffee—to coincide. Trash is not just thrown away, not just "something thrown before, or over against," but the concrete and material particulars, here of the idealist *Gegenstände*, sloughed off on the way to the Absolute, which in the context of Kant and Hegel at least in part entails the vindication of the subject's conceptual labor, ultimately at the expense of subject and object both. Is trash then still an obstacle—is it one to be overcome or one to which we submit?

Hegel's thought itself becomes an object for Adorno, as he uses it as an occasion to articulate his own version of the subject/object relationship: "No-one can read any more out of Hegel than he puts in. The process of understanding is a progressive self-correcting of such projections through comparison with the text. The content itself contains, as a law of its form, the expectation of productive imagination on the part of one reading" (Adorno 1993, 139). This is not solely a philosophical experience but also potentially and actually an *aesthetic* experience, as the reading subject projects, imagines, and speculates, comparing her own experience with the perception of the object. Adorno refers to this as "exact imagination," the coming together of the objective precision of truth and the imaginative agency of the subject, this latter characterized as aconceptual. To render it in the terms I have tried to trace, the truth of Hegel, like the truth of trash, is to be found in the imaginative recreation of an ungraspable totality, of which this page, that work, and these rags are a part.

Moreover, for all the trouble, fatigue, and even boredom the subject/object split has caused philosophers, nonetheless it can also provide a salutary litmus test for evaluating the extent to which philosophy, history, and society are all mutually imbricated. Adorno in his great essay "Subject and Object," reads as *true* the Idealist overcoming of the subject/object split under the rubric of identity—but not in the way that Hegel describes or intends it. Instead, such an enforced reconciliation under identity thinking merely underscores the pervasive power of reification: on the one hand, it attests to the evaporation of subjectivity, if not its coagulation into an object, and on the other hand, again, it confirms "the catastrophic spell of things," objects taking on uncanny lives of their own at our expense—ragpickers indifferently becoming rags, rags becoming ragpickers. Yet to consider the subject as simply—even naively—separate from the world accurately reflects the subject as alienated, even as such a consideration is false to the extent that it naturalizes and hypostatizes this separation and alienation, prescribing it as the limit of our engagement with the world. He writes, "Defining means that something objective, no matter what it may be in itself, is subjectively captured by means of a fixed concept. Hence the resistance offered by defining subject and object. To determine their meanings takes reflection on the very thing which definition cuts off for the very sake of conceptual flexibility. Hence the advisability, at the outset, of taking up the words 'subject' and 'object' as the well-honed philosophical language hands them to us as a historical sediment—not, of course, sticking to such conventionalism but continuing with critical analysis" (Adorno 1998, 246). Adorno resists a notion of objective—empirical, pragmatic—knowledge of the object, arguing in his best Nietzschean mode that if we think the object conceptually, we merely mistake our concept for the object, not realizing that we can only approach the object through the subject, in the process blinding ourselves to the particulars of the object that fall outside of conceptual thought. Moreover, the concepts of subject and object themselves emerge as if from the junk shop of philosophy, sedimented, as Adorno describes them, and well used, bearing the fingerprints of their history—not entirely dissimilar to the elements that comprise Benjamin's montage. But Adorno's solution is decidedly not Benjamin's: Adorno will insist upon the primacy of the object.

Adorno's argument for the primacy of the object stems from two points. First of all, here the object is ambivalently distinct from the Kantian thing-in-itself, which Adorno asserts commits us to skepticism, thus enabling the subsumption of the object to conceptual thought. Second, the primacy of the object entails and indeed *demands* a subject: "since primacy of the object requires reflection on the subject and subjective reflection, subjectivity—as distinct from primitive materialism, which really does not permit dialectics—becomes a moment that lasts" (Adorno 1998, 256). Consequently, this is *not* the bourgeois subject in the sense that the subject is *not* self-made and does *not* pull itself into existence by its bootstraps like Baron Munchausen but is rather the result of a dialectical engagement with objects. And subjectivity as a moment that lasts and as an object itself argues for the possibility of *social* engagement, a moment in which the subject can perceive herself as objectively determined by social processes. This leaves the subject "revealed to be a historical category, both the outcome of the capitalist process of alienation and a defiant protest against it" (Adorno 1991b, 249). This should not be mistaken for what Heidegger calls "thrownness," wherein *Dasein* must choose from among possibilities that are historically, socially, and culturally determined and choose either authentically or inauthentically—such an existential account remains for Adorno too indebted to idealism, since the possibility of an authentic choice for being-in-the-world depends on an agency and a social context unavailable in the unseasonable climate of late capitalism. Despite both the evident and subterranean parallels between the two thinkers, Adorno maintains that Heidegger provides an ontology to analyze problems that were better dealt with materially and historically. Thus he reads Heidegger as transposing the subject/object conflict onto the transcendent conceptual poles of *Dasein* and *Welt*. And this process leaves a remainder, "forlorn particulars that mock the conceptual, composed of minimal utensils, refrigerators, lameness, blindness, and the distasteful bodily functions. Everything waits to be carted off to the dump" (Adorno 1991b, 252). Here, Adorno's litany of garbage and shit serves as a salutary rebuke, not just to Heidegger, but also and ultimately to all modes of thought that in seeking to legislate over what is, neglect or ignore the trash at our feet—that trash that at every step shows up conceptual thought as necessarily incomplete, at best unfinished, at worst dominating.

We are back in the dump, not far from where we left Benjamin. His other famous trash heap occurs, of course, in his "Theses on the Philosophy of History," specifically in his reading of Paul Klee's "Angelus Novus," a passage that continues to invite commentary from generations of thinkers. But rather than go over that again, it might well prove more useful to argue that Benjamin had no monopoly on thinking redemption, even or especially of this qualified kind. Adorno's implacable critique, his forbidding prose and his mandarin attitudes often obscure his views on how both the reified subject and the world of objects may finally be changed and even redeemed. For he writes that it is the work of theory, of philosophy, to contemplate the ruins of the world as they would appear from the perspective of redemption. This is an impossible task for thought, says Adorno, but "[e]ven its own impossibility it must at last comprehend for the sake of the possible. But beside the *demand* thus placed on thought, the question of the reality or unreality of redemption hardly matters" (Adorno 1974, 247). It is the demand placed on thinking that is essential and as such never messianic, though such a demand can never come with a guarantee. This is a demand to think the rags like a ragpicker, to allow constitutive subjectivity to loosen like a bad tooth such that one might play at being an object. It is a demand to be like the object especially where that object falls outside of economies of thought and exchange—where it can be seen as scandalously particular and not merely "thrown over or against." It is to redeem trash, a task made all the more pressing by the seeming eclipse of art. That this is also a redemption of the object from its servitude to the subject therefore implies the redemption of the subject, too.

For Adorno, the products of the Culture Industry are junk and worse, never to be recovered or redeemed but only rejected, abjected, and tossed away. It is junk to be resisted, avoided, and critiqued, and, exceptionally, occasionally, it is junk to be alchemically transformed through the rigors of thought or modernist style into something of value. But this division between modernism and mass culture stands in for another: to the extent that culture under modernity bifurcates to produce such antinomies it becomes as well symptomatic of the very division of labor that underwrites its production, consumption, and, crucially, analysis. Of this last, an academic disciplinarity that

separates the critique of mass culture from the contemplation of canonical films merely reproduces this cultural division itself on the level of theory and institution, organizing
and managing academic labor according to instrumental
reason's strategies of integration and domination. To return
briefly to issues touched on earlier, film studies's division
along theory/posttheory lines itself articulates more than
mere preference for one mode of analysis over another and
less than the triumph of sober materialism over philosophi-
cal/theoretical excess. It reproduces in its very lineaments
many of these reductive oppositions, including some often
used to disparage Adorno: art versus entertainment, theory
versus praxis, molecular versus molar, and more besides.
Pointedly, theory's rejection of mass culture not only repli-
cates a stance as old as modernism and modernity but also
dialectically reveals how conservative and traditional views
of value, exchange, and equivalence can merely mask the
reification and negative integration of *academic* culture, an
integration in its larger social form largely blamed upon
the Culture Industry; and posttheory's disparagement of
film studies's rich theoretical history tends to reproduce in
another register the problems of all empirical/pragmatic
modes of thought, in which the concept is taken for the
thing itself, with the difference between the two consigned
to the junkyard. The resolution of such antinomies promises, of course, an essential freedom yet to come—but not
yet.

David Rodowick has called, persuasively and movingly,
for an elegy for theory.[9] The notion of the elegy as such
implies that theory, or at least a certain historical instantiation of it, is dead—that at best we can with all the dullness
of fusty professors attempt to sort out what is living from
what is dead in film theory. Yet one thing cinema tells us
again and again is that the dead are never dead, that they
will continue to be animated for us, whether in the mimetic
and ontological sense that Metz says obtains for most film,
or in the dutiful return of older seemingly obsolete genres,
or in the shape of remakes and sequels, or even in terms of
all the vampires and zombies themselves, cinematic figures

that persist in so very many ways after their passing—
figures of the persistence of the dead among the living.

But this is not the place to argue for a Derridean
"hauntology" for theory, whatever admitted appeal clings
to imagining the ghosts of Lacanians or Althusserians past
eerily wafting about cultural studies plenaries and cognitiv-
ist panels at the conference. If theory lives on, in however
liminal a fashion, it cannot be in the unstable, quasi-ideality
of the specter but only in the far more disturbing—and thus
arguably far more potent—form of trash. Such a claim for
theory remains here to be proven, but its relevance for art is
emphatic. Consider Adorno here writing on Kafka: "Kafka
sins against an ancient rule of the game by constructing art
out of nothing but the refuse of reality. He does not directly
outline the image of the society to come—for in his as in
all great art, asceticism to the future prevails—but rather
depicts it as a montage composed of waste-products which
the new order, in the process of forming itself, extracts from
the perishing present" (Adorno 1967b, 251–52). Again,
he intimates the alliance of art and garbage, although one,
unpromisingly enough, secured on the terrain of a canonical modernism. For Adorno, Kafka's innovation (if we want
to call it that) lies in part in his refusal of innovation and
the new, both in terms of his immanent materials and also
certainly in terms of his rejection of utopia, or indeed of
any world to come. Implicitly here and explicitly elsewhere,
Adorno's characterization of Kafka also comes to have implications for the status of history and narrative as such: these
waste products themselves block an imagining of the future,
deriving as they do from the exhaustion of the present. As
such, waste comes to join art (as I suggested in terms of
Kiss Me Deadly) in keeping faith with an anamnestic relation to past and present, including that work's prohibition
on images of a better world. It is because the present is being
consumed that the future cannot be construed; and the past,
which must have included a memory of something better,
finds itself reduced to garbage—"Made eternal, the transient is overtaken by a curse" (Adorno 1967b, 252). There

seems little enough room for memory in a now-perpetual present.

Inhospitable as a modernist context must be for *Repo Man*, it nonetheless evinces a fundamental sympathy for such a construal of history:

> MILLER. Suppose you were thinking about a plate of shrimp. Suddenly, someone will say "plate" or "shrimp" or "plate of shrimp." No explanation. No point in looking for one either. It's all part of the cosmic unconsciousness.
>
> I'll give you another instance. You know how everyone is into weirdness these days? Books in all the supermarkets about the Bermuda Triangle, UFOs, how the Mayans invented television? Well, the way I see it, it's exactly the same. There ain't no difference between a flying saucer and a time machine. People get hung up on specifics and miss out on seeing the whole thing.
>
> Take South America, for example. In South America, thousands of people go missing every year. Nobody knows where they go. They just, like, disappear. But if you think about it for a minute you realize something. There had to be a time when there was no people. Right? Well, where did all these people come from? I'll tell you where. The future. Where did all these people disappear to —Hmmm?
>
> OTTO. The past?
>
> MILLER. That's right! And how did they get there? Flying saucers. Which are really—yeah, you got it—time machines!

Miller (Tracey Walter), whom Otto (Emelio Estevez) suggests did a lot of acid in the 1960s, follows Kafka in abstaining from representing the future, as here it is only invoked as a point of departure, an antitelos, which would seem to imply that the future and the present are and will be somehow worse than the past. But then, of course, we know as Miller does not that the disappeared of South America are neither time travelers nor passengers on UFOs but rather executed political prisoners, whose murder cannot ever be thought of as an escape from history but rather as history's unequivocal instantiation (history being what hurts, as Jameson emphatically asserts).[10] For Miller then "weirdness"—conspiracy theories, occultism, UFO-ology, and other proto–New Age epistemologies

Figure 3.1   Miller and Otto

and spiritualties—can then be mustered to serve not a vision of totality, whether history itself or the unrepresentable and ungraspable system of global capital, but seemingly a wholesale retreat from history. But negatively Miller's bizarre epistemology also expresses a subterranean desire for history—what is, here, really a desire for a somehow more authentic present, or even for a future, with the implied proviso that that future not resemble this present. The present of the film, of this scene, consists of a custodian and an LA punk, standing around a burning barrel in a peripheral industrial wasteland, watching the flames consume (among other things) a sombrero, which can at best been registered as a grim and metonymic affirmation of those similarly consumed under a Pinochet. That is, if we can be bothered to notice, busy as we are chuckling at the effects of substance abuse—LSD and tabloids—on the imagination of this character.

On a more immanent level, Miller's reflections necessarily also reflect on the film itself, as well as on our investment in it: they express a desire for meaning, and meaning of a now-discredited global kind, for one of Lyotard's grand narratives to donate significance and shape to what seems always on the verge of collapsing into a heap of aleatory fragments. It is an assertion that sheer contingency—that "plate of shrimp"—is itself meaningful in the minimal and strictly formal function it serves. But finally we cannot think of the plate of shrimp as formally or thematically meaningful in that sense, as a post-modern variant, say, of Mallarmé's *Un Coup de Dés*, with *le hazard* now ambivalently overcome, or at least sublimated into a metaphysics or ontology. For as Napoleon and Lagarto Rodriguez (Eddie Velez and Del Zamora) stop outside a diner after stealing the 1964 Chevy Malibu that is here the object of everyone's desire, we see advertised in the window a "2.95 Plate-O-Shrimp Luncheon Special," as if to affirm Miller's "cosmic unconsciousness." However, it tells us rather more than that. It confirms that what from one vantage appears as contingency is really the principle of exchange value as such, that operation under which swarms of particulars come to be rendered undifferentiated and equivalent under money. It reveals contingency as necessity.

This is to say that Miller's vision both is and is not affirmed by the film—but more important, that his bricolage of a sus-pect kind of sense out of incommensurable and dubious, degraded and reactionary, discredited and trashy modes of thought and belief comes to rebound back upon the real of history itself, as out of this trash the atrocities of history come to be laterally glimpsed, as if in a dreamlike rebus, the disap-peared fleetingly made visible. The unimaginable deaths of thousands serves as an indictment of history itself and arrests our attempts to grasp history as meaningful in any fulsome way, as it can only now seem to us to be as occult, barbaric, and violent as the lurid images of the most threadbare air-port thriller or imaginatively bankrupt horror film, a matter of body counts. Or, indeed, as this postmodern mash-up of cultural detritus.

This is *Repo Man*'s open secret and strategy: that the junk of the present testifies not solely to the present as junk or worse, nor only to our abstention from imagining the future, nor yet to that future's impossibility, but rather to the idea that our way to a future that is not like the barbarity of the present can only be sifted out of the trash of the past, through its reclamation and redemption.

The film's credit sequence itself offers such an opportunity: on the one hand, its glossy computer font and images seem in an immanent sense to offer what the film will come to oppose—that is, the instrumental bureaucratic and scientific reduction of lived space into a high-tech simulacrum, the better to discipline and manage those who find themselves now reduced to data within it. And yet something like a Hegelian ruse of history infects a contemporary apprehension of this now antiquated technology—is this DOS? On a monochrome monitor no less? Far from signaling the airless voids of cyberspace or the ubiquity of surveillance, the sequence now testifies to little else than its own obsolescence, and in doing so hints at lines of flight that might have been invisible to the film's contemporary audience. For this is not *All the President's Men* (1976) or even *Three Days of the Condor* (1975), evoking the immaterial networks of global data and capital as in Jameson's bravura readings,[11] even though the film will come dutifully to mobilize all the figures of government or corporate conspiracy, offering Agent Rogersz (Susan Barnes) with her metal hand, crew of subordinates, and truck of computers and surveillance equipment, all bent on finding the mysterious Chevy Malibu. Here, though, the conspiracy never assumes the role of an epistemological or ontological principle—these agents are remarkably ineffective—but instead only functions to announce that *there is a conspiracy*, even, perhaps, that some sort of collective agency still exists in this utterly alienated world, no matter its repressive methods and instrumental form. According to the *OED*, the Latin *conspīrāre* literally means "to breathe together," whence "to accord, harmonize, agree, combine or unite in a purpose, plot mischief together secretly," and so gestures to the presence of a spirit distinct from those invoked in *Kiss Me Deadly*.

This may seem less of a theoretical stretch if we come to consider the persistent critique of Scientology on offer here, as in the climactic sequence, where two agents consider their favorite passages from their movement's foundational text,

Dioretix: The Science of Matter over Mind, a text Otto has already consigned to the flames of the trash can earlier:

> AGENT. God I love this job . . . It's more than a job, it's a call-
> ing. Why, you can say spiritual.
> AGENT WITH BANDAGED NOSE. Spiritual?
> . . .
> AGENT. Have you read this book? *Dioretix.*
> AGENT WITH BANDAGED NOSE. Chapter Seven. It's great.
> AGENT. I've got it marked.

While the glowing Malibu unleashes a lightning bolt to set fire to the Bible of the televangelist brought in to exorcise it (and this amid an unlikely shower of ice cubes), these two seek explicitly to emphasize the spiritual qualities of their work. Tempting as it is to speculate on what precisely the agent might mean, clearly enough for the film these two are as deluded as all the other workers here who imagine their jobs as vocations: Bud (Harry Dean Stanton) with his Repo Code, which we will turn to in a moment; Lite (Sy Richardson), who had earlier recommended *Dioretix* to Otto ("That book will change your life. Found It In a Maserati in Beverly Hills"); or Kevin (Del Zamora), for whom "[t]here's fucking room to move as a fry cook!" Spirit, then, extends from conspiracy as such to partake of everything that is fake, suspect, inauthentic, and ideological here in *Repo Man,* from covert government operations to vocational satisfaction, not to forget, of course, the Reverend Larry, whose televisual appeals have persuaded Otto's parents to give away his college fund. Spirit is trash.

Even so, such a characterization of spirit seems necessarily to entail a desire for, variously, collectivity, a vocation, and even a transcendental structure of belief. Otto's parents, never shown without a joint, seem incapable of affirming anything else, even if chronic hemp abuse lies at some distance from, say, the Hegelian *Weingeist* uncorked at the opening of *The Phenomenology,* when Hegel argues that "[t]he true is thus the bacchanalian frenzy, in which no member is sober" (Hegel 1977, 18)—spirit may be intoxicating, but intoxication is not necessarily spiritual. Similarly, while their devotion to the

Figure 3.2   Otto holding *Dioretix*

Rev. Larry's naked pleas for money suggest both a spiritual and social desire—after all, Otto's college money went to send Bibles to El Salvador—the film can bring itself to affirm little enough about these or indeed any other characters here.

But to characterize all these instantiations of spirit negatively—as is certainly the case here—is not to have done with it altogether or to affirm finally Miller's vision of the utter absence of meaning. Might it be that, like utopia, spirit can now only operate under a ban, as a true rationality in a world now wholly irrational, its reality preserved only by this restless cataloguing and subsequent negation of its inauthentic forms—that is, only by way of negation and contradiction— that it no longer has any immanence but must rather be inferred from a patient and seemingly endless denunciation of its false instantiations? But then we find ourselves in the terrain of a negative dialectic that then must confront its false and affirmative other, which the film helpfully names for us in a potently evocative condensation: *Dioretix: The Science of Matter over Mind*. Certainly this bogus spirituality invites laughter to the extent that the film reveals it as utterly true, as matter and the commodity form in particular have usurped all the prerogatives we might wish to associate with human consciousness and agency; and it's probably worth laboring the obvious joke that this text aims squarely at causing its adherents to soil their trousers, as this irrational welding of science to spirit also elevates the rate of urination—a way, one supposes, of chastising a consciousness that conceives of itself as sovereign and self-sufficient.

But a "science"—not an art or ethics!—of "matter over mind" might also conjure much more than it intends. If the subject is already a mere point of consumption, under the sway of commodity and capital, and if all formerly authentic collectivities have been effaced or replaced with more instrumental forms—if, in short, the mind is already wholly under the sway of matter, then *Dioretix* can only be an ideological justification after the fact, affirmative of what already exists— which indeed is what it appears to be. Moreover, as a science, even one of a pointedly suspect sort, Dioretix emphasizes the instrumental aspects of the subject/object relation: even as it reverses them, the principle of domination, formerly, of sovereign consciousness over recalcitrant matter, remains intact. But, of course, it is precisely this reversal of science and, indeed, positivism, on display here that augurs something else; for if the stance to be reversed by Dioretix—the historical domination of matter by mind and object by subject—can be identified with the dialectic of enlightenment itself, with the reduction of what is historically variable into a well-nigh metaphysical invariant and the promotion to a timeless "law" of past and present experiences over future possibilities, then at least this particular suspect ideology has the signal benefit of undoing the prescriptive aim of empirical and positivist sciences, which for Adorno is "the liquidation of the new, of the possibility that the facts might change" (Jarvis 1998, 88). As nakedly false and ideological as it is, Dioretix nonetheless suggests that the subject/object relationship might be transformed.

As Adorno writes, "the dialectical problem of ideologies [is] that these are indeed false consciousness, but that they are nevertheless not only false" ("Contribution to the Theory of Ideology," qtd. in Jarvis 1998, 65). Thus *Dioretix: The Science of Matter over Mind* is neither just false nor only utopian—and hence impossible and equally ideological. It also constitutes a promise of the passing of an instrumental domination of matter and nature. Adorno continues, "We can only talk meaningfully about ideology in so far as something spiritual [*ein Geistiges*] comes forward from the social process as independent, substantial and with its own claim. Its untruth is always the price of just this separation, the denial of its social ground. But its truth-moment also adheres to just this independence, to a consciousness which is more than the mere impression of what exists, and which therefore strives to penetrate what exists. Today the characteristic mark of ideologies is the absence of this independence, rather than a deceptive claim to independence" ("Contribution to the Theory of Ideology," qtd. in Jarvis 1998, 65–66). Humorous, even absurd as such a science/spirituality is, it nonetheless attests to spirit—that is, to a sense in which matter, whether hypostasized by empiricism and positivism or granted an uncanny vitality by the commodity form, offers an occasion for free speculation and for imagining how the relationship between mind and matter, subject and object, might come to be transformed.

A science of matter over mind then not only is false but also attests to a desire to think of subject and object otherwise, in terms at a remove from the objectified subjects and trashy objects that populate the film. But it is also the case that such transformations of mind, single and collective, have been effected on matter, too, as the sovereign form that such matter takes here is the commodity: cars, but also the generic cans of "food" and "drink," which seem to be without the need for a subject to donate to them the power they so evidently wield. The commodity as Lukácsian second nature already determines mind; and what is needed, then, the truth that this joke both aims at and misses, is another way of conceiving the relationship of matter and mind—a thought from an impossible outside that assays an escape from the gravitational pull of this second nature.

Let's return to the credit sequence, to the primitive computer image that draws our attention to Route 66, Los Alamos, and Roswell, historical and cultural names that coalesce into a crucial constellation of images. In Jameson's examples, networking technology is mobilized as a privileged figure of economic and geographical totality (Jameson 1992), though here Miller's big picture—"the whole thing"—is ultimately to be thought of as secondary to the "specifics." That is, the dialectic is properly negative, as the big picture can only ever be provisional, when it is not irredeemably suspect due to its implication in historical and economic violence. Pop-cultural escape—a place where you can "get your kicks"—nuclear apocalypse, and the entanglement of extraterrestrials and government conspiracy provide an elementary constellation fully as geopolitical as it is escapist. That is, these three terms also minimally evoke a dialectic of their own, one in which escape—to the West or to the stars—is intuited as desirable and even necessary in the awful light of Los Alamos, not the last reminder of *Kiss Me Deadly* this film will conjure. It will be here that we come to be introduced to this film's preeminent uncanny object, one that will punningly vehiculate various transitions from genre to genre, scene to scene, character to character, subject to object, and one that will bind together and instantiate these elementary coordinates, and ultimately, desperately, attempt to hint at their overcoming: a 1964 Chevy Malibu.

The Malibu, driven by J. Frank Parnell (Fox Harris), is pulled over in a speed trap, and on opening the trunk the state trooper is vaporized by a blast of white light, which leaves only his boots smoking in the desert dust.[12] In this manner *Repo Man* starts at the end of *Kiss Me Deadly*, recapitulating that film's apocalyptic finale as if to imagine what follows the apocalypse, what comes after that end of history. But if in that earlier film the Great Whatsit attempted to embody art's impossible autonomy, its savage judgment and condemnation of a culture that no longer had any place for it, here all seems played for laughs. It is rather to the contents of this vehicle that our attention is directed, both in terms of its driver, made mad for his part in inventing the neutron bomb, and what lurks in its trunk, which turns out to be the unstable and decaying bodies of aliens, stolen from a secret base in Roswell. Its deadly aura evokes not distance, as in Benjamin's construal of the work of art, but a lethal proximity, and this despite its extraterrestrial cargo. That is, even with its reflexivity, its antiauthoritarian and otherworldly aspects, this glowing box retains little enough of the critical and demiurgic power that it evinced in Aldrich's film. A 1964 Chevy Malibu seems no dream of an impossibly autonomous work of art.

But what then is it? Certainly a commodity—but as the film shows us a multiplicity of ways in which this commodity—the car—articulates a particular set of values, this Malibu remains stubbornly distinct. As Otto gets further enmeshed in the occupation of repo man, the film offers no end of cars, each coming to speak to a variety of ways in which this specific commodity offers illusory opportunities for various consumers to distinguish themselves based on their "individual" taste: Otto himself will come to drive an outrageous Eldorado;[13] he will repossess a number of luxury cars and sports cars, BMW's and Porsches; and the other repo men also offer insights into their own characters based on the cars they drive. Fundamentally Otto's very name puns on the primary identity obtaining here between the individual and his commodity choice. Your choice of car cannot evoke your unique subjectivity—an impossible task for a mass-produced commodity—but rather it affirms how you are your car. Otto is an auto, an exchangeable commodity shuttled among various agencies and consumers, a thing to them and to himself. This both binds him and only minimally distinguishes him from the other repo men, whose own names—Bud, Oly, Miller, Lite—are all taken from beers. And yet, dialectically, even this rebarbative and minimal identity serves to distinguish Bud, Oly, Miller, and Lite from the commodities everywhere on display in the convenience stores they frequent, in which all beverages are "drink"—they at least have the dignity of a brand name. Oly's joke on meeting Otto—"Otto? Otto parts?"—does more, though, than make plain an already evident pun: it also poses a different question to constitutive subjectivity, of which the film's fascination with the commodity form is itself a part, asking after the elements out of which such a subject is made. If the Malibu comes to be an exemplary illustration of the "mysteries" of exchange value and commodity fetishism, how such a mundane object can come to be possessed by an enigmatic and uncanny allure, it also asserts the object status of all who seek to possess it.

This can be affirmed the other way round as well, and in a manner that responds to the opportunity opened by Dioretix: Bud educates Otto in the "Repo Code," saying, "I shall not cause harm to any vehicle nor the personal contents thereof, nor through inaction let that vehicle or the personal contents thereof come to harm. That's what I call the repo code, kid. Don't forget it, etch it in your brain. Not many people got a code to live by anymore." In Chapter 1, I suggested how Sam Spade's own ethical code, invoked to guarantee his status as a unique individual against the oppressive inauthenticities of legal and criminal worlds alike, serves ultimately to alienate himself from himself. But now in *Repo Man* ethics and individual both can only be parsed ironically, as the subject seems only to exist in order to serve the object, which now determines and deforms relations between subjects. Here Bud functions as a voice of experience, whose authority derives, we infer, from his many years as a repo man—what has his experience to teach us? First, precisely that experience as a basis for knowledge and ethics is the experience of commodities. Surely the humor of Bud's system inheres in the extent to which it outlines not an interpersonal ethics but an ethics of the object, and therefore of the utter irrelevance or impossibility of conceiving of how one subject might relate to another. Here matter—the car—has supplanted mind.

And yet dialectically we might have good use for an ethics of the object, if not the one that Bud here espouses, dependent as it is on maintaining the commodity's reign uncontested. In another context, thinkers as disparate as Stanley Cavell and Gilles Deleuze orient film's goal in ethical terms, suggesting (albeit in very different ways) how film provides an antidote to skepticism and a faith in the possibilities of change in the real.[14] Such an understanding of ethics skews sharply from what it still seems necessary to interrogate as bourgeois ethics, from Marx to Weber and Adorno, in which

self-preservation and the repudiation of pleasure—what
work demands under capitalism—come to be affirmed as
moral virtues by a society that "needs a moral ideology of
the individual and his renunciation of happiness to sustain
itself in its own injustice" (Adorno 1993, 49). As Bud says,
"Guys who make it are the guys who get into their cars at any
time. Get in at three A.M., get up at four. That's why there
ain't a repo man I know that don't take speed." Insofar as
Repo Man is also Otto's *bildungsroman*, it can only be a negative one: his "formation" is not composed of moral or psychological growth, or even of progressive socialization, but
rather of the cumulative rejection of all these things, such
that the process of *bildung* itself stands revealed as nothing
less than the effect of social and economic rationalization.
Otto restlessly moves from one authority figure to another
in his "narrative of development": from the family, because
his father has donated his college fund to a television evan-
gelist, from the fatuous pieties of his boss at the supermar-
ket, from the incoherent and ideological views of the various
repo men, from the indifferent and immature "relationships"
he has with Debbie and Leila, finally to "maturity," which,
typically, emerges at the end of the narrative itself and, as
we shall see, takes on a very particular form here. As Franco
Moretti tells us, *bildung* coincides with the transformations
demanded of its subject by the processes of technological
and economic change—capital itself (Moretti 2000). Maturity, wisdom—the payoff, narratively and psychically, of this
form—stand exposed as a wholesale ideology of the defor-
mation and management of youthful desire by changes in
the mode of production; and what seemed a narrative of the
winning of wisdom and experience, with the merest shift of
perspective becomes a "humanist" allegory of nonhuman
powers. What was to have been the subject's emergence is
revealed as its eclipse. Otto will quite properly refuse this
narrative of maturity, particularly the ambivalent benefits
of marriage, which typically provides a culmination to the
process of *bildung* and comedy alike: before he gets into the
Malibu at the film's climax, Leila, who we should remember

has tortured him, asks, "What about our relationship?" to which Otto replies, "Fuck that."

So *Repo Man* offers not an ethics of a world to come, here merely a point of departure to the past, nor an ethics of work, nor a social or a personal ethics, but an ethics of the object. André Bazin is relevant here: as Prakash Younger argues, "[a]t the root of Bazin's ontological argument one can discern the assumption of an inescapable ethical dimension to human life and culture, one which simultaneously secures the illuminations of art and the skeptical awareness of ideology" (Younger 2003). That is, Bazinian ontology—the ability of film art to present and represent being-in-the-world—is or should be ethically bound to do justice to its objects. That this aim always fails—hence the evocation of ideology here—comes to stand in Younger's reading of Bazin for the necessity of error and ideology themselves as waypoints along the asymptotic approach to the real. While it would be reductive to identify the object of the Bazinian real with nature itself, our context here—the utterly commodified world of *Repo Man*—suggests the lack of availability not just of nature, nowhere present in the industrial peripheries of LA, but of anything not already stamped and sealed by exchange value. The only reality here can be the reality of exchange, of consumption and so of alienation and reification, all of which work to affirm not some more profound or authentic world beneath the blandishments of ideology but rather the dispiriting conclusion that this is all there is. The strictures of exchange govern all relationships here, between objects and subjects, leaving no space, geographical or temporal, that might afford that longed for yet impossible vantage from which it might have been possible to discern the Bazinian real beneath.

The exception is trash, which litters the frame virtually throughout. Trash testifies to a reality that subtends the gleaming cars, the shelves of "food" and "drink," its insistent presence an obstacle to taking the commodity at face value. After repossessing a red Cadillac, Otto pursues Leila running on the street and tries to pick her up, only to crash into a bunch of brimming garbage cans. Trash, in its obdurate materiality, here deflates the pretensions and status the Cadillac was thought to confer, even suggesting its future as scrap. The film thus binds itself to the truth of trash by being true to trash, both in its choice of generic materials and in giving it an image.

But this is not yet the ethics of the object for which we have been prepared; a fuller elaboration depends on the opportunities afforded by these two realities, car and trash, which coincide in the Malibu itself. Its scandal, for us as much as for the characters, inheres in the ascription of value to it: a fax to the repo office says Double X Finance has put $20,000 in escrow for its repossession, an amount that both inspires and bewilders the repo men as well as their antagonists, the Rodriguez brothers. Here the Malibu becomes specific through an unfathomable contradiction: how could a piece of junk be worth $20,000? Having little enough use, it thus seems to be a thing of utter exchange value, but it is decidedly not a Porsche or El Dorado: it is neither new nor "classic," neither a commodity precisely nor an antique. The specificity of the 1964 Chevy Malibu—its elevation and particularity compared not just to the other vehicles here but also to all other 1964 Chevy

Figure 3.3   Otto and trash

Malibus—is thus mediated through contingency and social specificity—which is to say that its status as a "work of art," its very singularity and sensuous immediacy, its hermetic interior (filled with auratic aliens!) and thing-like exterior alike (and could there be a trashier example given, this side of a Trabant?)[15] all go to demonstrate, perhaps more effectively, finally, than the Great Whatsit, the extent to which the work of art's notional and longed-for autonomy coincides with the commodity itself. Eschewing use value, being-for-society, it embodies sheer exchange value, its autonomy now revealed as a homeopathic adoption of the commodity form against that form, bought at the outrageous price of its uselessness. Adorno writes, "The absolute artwork converges with the absolute commodity," and if the new in Baudelaire was "the aesthetic seal of expanded reproduction, with its promise of undiminished plenitude" (Adorno 1997, 21) now the old—junk and garbage—shows that plenitude in its negative form, shows its cost, even as *Repo Man*'s aspirations to the absolute must be distinguished from those of *Les Fleurs du Mal*. The Malibu stands undistinguished but unapproachable, quotidian and exceptional, junk and valuable all at once.

Here, punctually, the question of reification again arises, a necessary and indispensable dialectical counterpart to the problems of commodification everywhere rehearsed in the film and brought to a head by this car. Yet surely *Repo Man* puts a crucial twist to this problem, too; for, given the omnipresence of the commodity here, along with the ample testimony offered regarding its effects on subjectivity, the salutary shock that *Repo Man* comes to provide for its critic inheres in the extent to which reification seems absent as a problem. As Timothy Bewes points out in his intensive historicization of reification, as a concept it always entails anxiety over reification; and in the absence of such anxiety the problem itself dissolves (Bewes 2002). Thus in a world in which the processes of commodification and reification are complete the problem vanishes—becoming object, the subject loses her critical vantage from which to lament the process.

Thus *Repo Man*'s is a world in which both subject and object have withdrawn, and neither seem available for thought, except in the form of Dioretix, a nearly naked ideology that nonetheless expresses a desire for those categories to be available again, reconfigured. Alienation and reification distort the subject, while exchange value and, more broadly, conceptual thought diminish the object. But it is precisely here that trash returns with a vengeance: Otto, already liminal due to his status as an unemployed punk at the outset, is virtually already an object even before his ambivalent apprenticeship as a repo man; and the panoply of cars on display here come to express in the very sequence of their presentation a paradoxical trajectory, for as we shift from El Dorado and Porsche to Malibu—from luxury car to junker—exchange value *increases*. For to be a repo man here is to assume one of Adorno's key tenets, as expounded in *Negative Dialectics*: that the object has priority. And what this then entails for a conception of subjectivity needs to be expressed in two ways: first, that such a priority does not entail a mere reversal of the Idealist primacy of the subject, for indeed such an illusory and fraught priority of the object is already in place, as the subject here has already become an object to itself, subject to the objects of the market; but second, the priority of the object must be subjectively recognized as mediated and not invariant. That is, a granting of priority to the object entails a recognition of its mediation. Adorno writes, "Only for subjective reflection, and for subjective reflection on the subject, is the priority of the object attainable . . . Mediation of the object means that it must not be statically, dogmatically hypostatized but can be known only as it entwines with subjectivity; mediation of the subject means that without the moment of objectivity it would be literally nil" (Adorno 1973, 185–86).

Mediation—dialectics!—in contrast to conceptual thought enables the subject to acknowledge its own moment of nonidentity, to conceive of its own objectivity as being both socially and historically produced as well as irreducible. It would be to acknowledge that the auto was made of parts after all and that some of those parts, especially the ones diminished as trash, as merely contingent or useless, might instead be seen as bringing the subject back to itself. The asymmetric mediation of subject and object enables those forlorn particulars, the remnants of conceptual thought and exchange, to be more than discarded fragments and to be seen as related to other particulars, elements in a historically encrusted constellation—rather than undifferentiated garbage in the dump.

In the film's rather more concrete terms, then, Otto become subject when he becomes a passenger—rather than a repossessor—of the Malibu, when he becomes able to experience it in all its complexity, even its magic, and abandons possessing it in economic or conceptual terms, when he relaxes his subjective sense of agency with its implied prerogative over objects, and when he allows its objectivity to mediate his sense of himself. In so doing, the Malibu's own fundamental and contradictory strangeness, its irreducible alterity, its noumenal richness—its essence—necessarily appears; and this, too, is the point—the moment at which the dioretic becomes negative, preserving the particularity of subject and object both while illustrating a new relationship between them—at which the promise of Dioretix *comes true*, in a manner distinct from the reduction of the subject to an alienated object. Its alien cargo, now forgotten, nonetheless still provides a science-fictional motor for the "sublation" of the older subject/object paradigm, as the car comes to levitate and then accelerate over a spectacular LA skyline, the lights of which, smearing and stretching in our vision due to the speed, fittingly echo Kubrick's *2001* (as well as reminding us of Miller's history with psychedelics), as this object and these subjects, mediating each other, come to be a constellation themselves in their transcendence of this world and their flight through the improbably clear LA atmosphere. *Dioretix: The Science of Matter over Mind* reverses from deception, mere ideology, and false consciousness into a glimpse of the subject and object reconciled. As Otto says and could only say here, "This is intense!"

But if it is intense, a Malibu is also not a time machine, at least in Miller's sense, and it is instead—it can only be—a

Figure 3.4   The auratic Malibu

work of art, and one, having withdrawn into an enigmatic and junky form, that has sought to evoke its own sublation of sheer exchange value, commodification, and the promise of happiness (which, pointedly, is not to be found in this world but necessarily beyond it—in the sky and after the film's own narrative closure). The Malibu's role, then, its counterintuitive self-designation as a work of art, entails a mimesis of the commodity form and rationalization broadly speaking: like the hermetic and withdrawn modernist work, this object, too, has taken in, of necessity, elements of the commodity form as a kind of pharmakon. If, as I argue in Chapter 1, the Maltese Falcon emerges as singular out of an irrational, mythic history and so comes to imply another kind of rationality, here that process extends, and our figure for the work of art—the Malibu—has not only emerged as a commodity, and a shabby one at that, but also as technical and technological, to no little extent even more rational than the dominated world from which it emerges. Art, emerging from myth, assumes a technological form all the more to rebuke the use of technology for domination, as well as to keep its magical origins alive in an utterly

disenchanted world. Just like the torturous temporality of
Miller's flying saucer/time machine, the work of art must
deploy the resources of the present to affirm its origins in
the past; but unlike the flying saucer there is no going back
to a time before disenchantment, for art, too, recognizes its
own role in the progressive secularization of magic even as
it keeps alive, anamnestically, a memory of that magic. As
in *Kiss Me Deadly*'s meditations on technology and art, this
is as potent an argument for the aesthetic power of film as
one might desire.

Given, though, the distance between more autonomous
or canonically validated works of art (as well as their own
filmic figures for themselves) and a 1964 Chevy Malibu
with aliens in its trunk, flying magically over the city carry-
ing an LA punk and a drug-damaged custodian, my claim
that the car and thus the film aspires to art might stand
in need of further proof. In *Kiss Me Deadly* particularly,
and in *The Big Lebowski* as we shall soon come to see, the
specificity of privileged objects, those that stand in for
the autonomous work of art, is tested in a context provided by a panoply of other aesthetic modes and forms.
Both of these films listlessly cite painting, dance, music,
performance, and others modes, restlessly searching for the
novum in historical contexts seemingly inimical to it. *Repo
Man* offers no such encyclopedic array of older or current
aesthetic modes—presumably most of them have already
been junked—but it does offer at least a couple of meditations on aesthetic value that might contribute here. Meeting Leila and Agent Rogersz at a punk bar, Otto reflects on
the performance of the Circle Jerks: "I can't believe I used
to like these guys" he laments, while they perform a truly
awful and very funny lounge version of one of their signature
songs, "When the Shit Hits the Fan," all the while sporting lurid blue tuxedos. While I might really want to read
this in terms of Adorno's "The Aging of the New Music,"
we might benefit from noting only that, like Schoenberg
and the 12-tone system itself, the novelty and avant-garde
blast that was West Coast punk in this period also comes,
here, to recognize its own aging and even exhaustion, its

novelty reduced to dogma and even hated tradition in the space of a couple of years. But of course punk was never only—or even centrally—concerned with novelty—that is, with either modernist innovation or with fashioning new forms for the marketplace, however construed. Instead, its own truth content derived from its critical negativity, particularly regarding the cultural marketplace—the Culture Industry—itself. Thus from "Destroy All Music" by the Weirdos, to Johnny Rotten's homemade "I Hate Pink Floyd" T-shirt, to the Circle Jerks' own penchant for punk defacements of popular songs, punk sought to use music against music, its repetitive and reduced means against a reduced and repetitive and utterly affirmative popular culture, so to become a wailing, expressive protest, devoid of romantic ornament and commodity sheen alike, against the timelessness and depthlessness of its contemporary culture, wholly commodified. It's not even an irony, though, that such negativity's fate was to be swiftly absorbed into the very marketplace it rejected, its forms and techniques become dogma as entrenched as the perennial and transhistorical "value" of the Beatles. What this means for our immanent context is that the Circle Jerks know what Otto does not yet—that their art is already in the process of ossifying into a mere series of poses and products for sale and that the only way to avoid this fate is to turn that same parodic negativity once directed at, say, the Carpenters (the Circle Jerks also cover "Close to You") against themselves and against punk, now seemingly fully as mechanical as anything on the Top Forty. In this sense, then, it signals resignation, as the expressive subject can no longer compel either material or form to embody the critical negativity that was once its prerogative. This performance recognizes the moment of punk's own passing and, with it, the passing of its aim to blast apart commodity music. It functions as an immanent critique but, unlike the Malibu, no more than that.

The other context available here entails a shift in registers, as it demands of its audience an attention not only to the contents of the frame but also to the frame itself—to the cinematography of Robby Müller. If the film ceaselessly cites many genres, if its episodic structure frustrates a more classical narrative continuity, and if its dependence upon the car, speed, and travel send it careening from one place and one episode to another, nonetheless Müller's cinematography provides more than merely a structural or aesthetic counterpoint. Indeed, among this chaos Müller's camera remains serene, offering an almost classical allegiance to composition and duration, rejecting inserts of all types in an effort to produce or to find a principle of continuity adequate for the materials on hand. One example might be compelled to serve: when for the third time Otto and Bud enter a convenience store to buy some beer, they are interrupted by Duke and Debbie on their crime spree, and the comic carnage of the ensuing sequence stands qualified by the classical impassivity of the camera, as well as by the transformation of the store's harsh fluorescents into something altogether more luminous, even numinous. Predictably enough the shootout ends in a bloodbath, with Duke dying on the floor as Otto cradles his head:

> DUKE. The lights are growing dim. I know a life of crime led me to this sorry fate. And yet I, I blame society. Society made me what I am.
> OTTO. That's bullshit. You're a white suburban punk, just like me.
> DUKE. But it still hurts.

Surrounded by "food" and "drink," dying from a shotgun blast, Duke produces a litany of clichés to account for his life, a litany whose lack of creativity echoes his line that serves at a headnote to this chapter: "Let's go get sushi and not pay!" Such a place and such a character preclude a heroic death by fiat; and yet as Müller's camera glides in to this face, this face of a character without imagination but also without opportunities, hope, or any sense of how the world might be other than it is, the image's restrained intimacy amid the strangely pure white light works to affirm if not his story then at least his suffering, which upon reflection proves to be, along with its earlier evocation of the disappeared, a moment of truth—but only a moment—in a film with little enough interest in truth in that sense.[16] The Malibu might offer an opportunity to reconcile subject and object, but it does not and cannot give expression to suffering.

And speculatively, what would it mean to ascribe Duke's dying words not solely to this cartoonish character but to the work of art—that "uncommitted crime"—itself? For Adorno "[e]very work of art is an uncommitted crime" (Adorno 1974, 111) because it challenges the social laws of labor and value: outrageously, it would seek to provide an instantiation of a labor that is free and of a value beyond exchange. It finds itself compelled to assume ever more provocative and enigmatic forms and modes because of its social opposition, its entanglement in the market, and so compounds its crime. Indeed, society has made it what it is: something that dies on the convenience store floor. But the crime remains uncommitted insofar as art is not to be identified with praxis—its transgressions and its promises cannot be realized in the social world without that world's prior transformation. Formerly, under modernity, art aspired to an autonomy that was to have been a precondition for such a transformation; now, "the lights are growing dim." And it still hurts.

Adorno begins his essay "Cultural Criticism and Society" by railing against the very term *Kulturkritik*, which like *automobile* embodies a contradiction, first in its lexical violence, mashing together Greek and Latin, and second, in its surreptitious implication that the critic exists at a magisterial remove from the object, culture (1967a, 19). Of course, the automobile also exemplifies another division, as the products of the Fordist production line that made the automobile viable emerge with sufficient illusory autonomy to grant them their fetishistic sheen, their aura, even a deceptively noumenal status, while simultaneously the worker is further divided from her labor, from herself. What this means for us here, particularly in seeking to describe the priority of the object and its implications for subject, art, and commodity, is that the object, like the Ford off the assembly line or the alien Malibu, cannot be construed as an invariant, since to do so would affirm it as an unconditioned ground and hence metaphysical. Alternatively, from the Kantian perspective on the object we considered earlier, the object as it appears to consciousness, submitted to conceptual labor, denies the object its due and value, implying instead that the conceptual activity of the subject produces it, a subject that from this perspective now appears as undetermined and self-constituting and so equally as metaphysical as the object. Culture and the car, even the culture of the car, must then be conceived not as invariants but as objects in process, as must the subject: specifically for it even to be possible for the subject to conceive of the object's priority the subject cannot be thought to be self-identical but rather nonidentical with itself, characterized by, even possessed by, an excess that demands recognition. Duke at the moment of his death comes to recognize himself as nonidentical in this sense, as a product of social forces; but Otto has come to see this already in his progressive sloughing off of social roles—stock boy, son, punk, repo man—and has moreover come to accept what is other as other, as the Malibu finally intimates a relation to the object that does not entail mastery, its subsumption under conceptual thought or exchange value, that does not entail calling it a *Gegenstände*, a commodity or a noumenon, but that instead entails a recognition of its particularity as well as of his own mediation by and through it. Not as a driver or an owner, let alone a repossessor, but as a passenger does Otto achieve his freedom—a reconciliation that can exist only in and as art, and a freedom whose very image and imagining can only be evoked through junk, after the trashing of the subject, beyond the pieties of aesthetic value, through the obsolete commodity.

CHAPTER 4

"JACKIE TREEHORN TREATS OBJECTS LIKE WOMEN!"

TWO TYPES OF FETISHISM IN *THE BIG LEBOWSKI* (1998)

> In psycho-analysis nothing is true except the exaggerations.
> —Theodor Adorno, *Minima Moralia*

It is the hardest thing in the world to be a materialist. In theory, that is—as a theorist. Even though thought seems irreducible in its linguistic and even imagistic materiality, nonetheless, an irreducible kernel of abstraction, idealism, and metaphysics always persists, like a mote—or a splinter—in the eye. Some of the current impasses in cultural studies might be compelled to resolve themselves around this subterranean persistence of essence concealed beneath appearance, as the concrete, lived experiences of classed and gendered bodies nonetheless bring to our very attempt to think them a troublesome abstraction, like baggage, trailing in their wake. But this claim might also allow another approach to these issues. The essentializing aspects of, say, gender and even of film itself then demand a mode of thought that might use the concept, thought, against itself, allowing subject and object to show forth their particularities without assimilating them to the determinants of a preexisting schema. Hence negative dialectics: for in the hic et nunc of late capitalism, essence can only be the current mode of production itself, while appearance, predictably enough, comes to represent the social relations of production.[1] Here the dialectic cuts both ways, giving a material density to philosophical abstraction while simultaneously making available to a critical materialism the rich conceptual history of a seemingly incompatible idealist philosophical history and tradition.

However, this would all be academic in that worst sense were it not for the extent to which this provisional formula can itself be rewritten in a more contemporary theoretical idiom, in a bid, to begin with, to historicize Adorno himself, whose own moment was a modernist one. This becomes necessary, too, to the extent that under postmodernism appearance now *is* essence: with postmodernism's fascination with surfaces and images of all varieties, the former opposition of essence and appearance is itself now mere appearance. Moreover, appearance stands not just for the reification of the social world but, as Adorno would doubtless remind us, also of the world of ideas, philosophy, theory, and film studies, too, now all but given over to disciplinarity and specialization. But appearance cannot fail to evoke its opposite, whatever that might now be: "What is, is more than it is. This 'more' is not imposed upon it but remains immanent to it, as that which has been pushed out of it. In that sense, the nonidentical would be the thing's own identity against its identifications" (Adorno 1973, 161). Identification, conceptualization, and apprehension, then, do more than compel the thing to appear; they seek to empty the object of what is more than appearance, and so to impose an identity, false as it is. The question then resolves itself like this: if appearance now is essence, if there now seem few enough opportunities or even reasons to worry after the niceties of anything other than appearance, then all the things of the world—not to except the subject—come to seem infinitely exchangeable, commodities all. But of course worries there are: for the violence that inheres in emptying objects of their superfluous "excess" visits the subject, too.

Dialectics speaks for this excess: "The name of dialectics says no more, to begin with, than that objects do not go into their concepts without leaving a remainder . . . [Contradiction] indicates the untruth of identity, the fact that the concept does not exhaust the thing conceived" (Adorno 1973, 5). If in considering *Repo Man* this remainder was rendered stubbornly visible as trash, now it is that we will come to think of this relation itself—of concept and object—as resolving into something other than either the domination of the object or the reduction of the subject. For what Adorno's thought might share with psychoanalysis—that still controversial science of the subject—can be traced precisely along the course described by the object itself; for it is in Lacan and Freud *das ding* that intrudes in its maddening, noumenal being, presenting a challenge to our ability to tame it conceptually. Outside of language and the unconscious, *das ding*, in at least its primary context, "is characterized by the fact that it is impossible for us to imagine it" (Lacan 1992, 125).[2]

Slavoj Žižek, the contemporary thinker perhaps most closely identified with both the dialectical method and psychoanalysis, would likely recast appearance/essence so as to argue that their opposition, at first, constitutes a stupid stereotype, a cliché.[3] His next move would be to uncover through analysis a hidden essence uniting the pair, to be followed by a return to the reality of dumb appearance as such, but now a dumb appearance that has been transformed into something far removed from both the immediately given object or opposition and from the analyzed and interpreted essence: the return to "dumb appearance" is now exposed as an undermining of empiricism, various crude materialisms, and the second-stage interpretation itself, which now stands revealed as always already having been a part of the object in its initial moment.[4] For Žižek, such a recasting of the dialectic has among its advantages an eschewal of synthesis or sublation while adhering to the tripartite form of the Hegelian dialectic.[5] Žižek's revision of the dialectic cannot be dismissed as mere postmodern play, nor should it be thought of as yet (just!) another rereading of Hegel; for particularly when cultural studies of all sorts seems to rely on its objects and phenomena as given in one moment, a moment later, demystified through critique, their essences revealed, it too often stops short of realizing that unity of theory and praxis to which it aspires. We might then have good reason for suggesting that critique is insufficient when it stops at exposing the ideological-racist-sexist essence of contemporary culture; and the problem deepens, as we shall see, when we consider the changes wrought on the work of art itself, when it comes to seem distinct from its bourgeois moment in which such a critique was pertinent and even possible. Žižek demands we take the next step and return to appearance, which in its very persistence presents a dumb challenge not only to the unity and elegance of theory's smart methods but also to theory's magisterial remove, its pretensions of objectivity when confronted with the object. This demand echoes Adorno's own emphasis in *Negative Dialectics* on the particularity of the object—especially the aesthetic object—as that which challenges categorical thought, associated not just with Kant but also inevitably with capitalism and the administered world, the hegemony of exchange value and identity thinking.[6] More specifically for feminism, the work of art's energies derive from the disjunction between it and the world, entailing a critique of the power and oppression that maintain that world; but this lack of fit also implies a utopian and emancipatory role for art.[7] The object in its psychic register might come to donate some of its frustrating resistance to the social domain, in which objects circulate seemingly frictionlessly; to turn the commodity into the Thing—*das ding*—might offer opportunities for object and subject both.

The Coen Brothers' cult film *The Big Lebowski* (1998) seems little more than appearance in some sense and has become a privileged exemplar of postmodernism in film due to its aleatory plot, parasitic relation to preexisting styles and genres, reduction of character to stereotype, and insistence on sheer visual surface. To my mind, the funniest—the most critical and ultimately utopian—moment occurs during the Dude's (Jeff Bridges) interrogation by the Malibu police chief. When he is warned off, told that Jackie Treehorn (Ben Gazzara) is a respected member of the community and so merits the scrupulous consideration of the police, the Dude, groggy from being drugged by the pornographer, responds with incredulity, "Jackie Treehorn treats objects like women, man!"

Of course the Dude is part of culture and not one who studies it as such; but his outburst's intent—if not its literal expression—embodies an economical critique if not a critique of economics, asserting objectification as the essence of pornography as appearance. The Dude's response is also both an articulation of and a provisional solution to the problem of fetishism. But before we get there, let me state the obvious: our initial laughter derives from the Dude's stoned inversion of what is often maligned as "political correctness." In attempting to demonstrate his opposition to the objectification of women by pornography, he instead makes evident his own desubjectification, his virtual objectification by drugs—he is unable to express his principles; they come out in an inverted form; he is not the master of his discursive domain. His ability to make a moral assertion and take a principled stand comes undone because of, we imagine, both the drug administered to him by Treehorn and the self-administered pot. Our amusement also derives from the lack of fit between an expression of outrage at pornography and the Dude's hemp-fuelled, Cali-mellow passivity—"The Dude abides" is his final and perhaps most characteristic self-description.[8] And, not incidentally, our laughter appears to have much to do with our rejection of and even contempt for cliché and dogma, even—or especially—when it is meant to express a principled and engaged position.

But surely our laughter expands, too, because of our perception of the truth inherent in this inversion: Treehorn's pimp-luxurious, Hefner-esque rooms suggest a man in love with things as well as a man who sees and profits from women as things. In this sense we might come to gloss the Dude's outburst also as a shrewd assertion of the problem of commodity fetishism and its links with sexism. As such, his stoned spoonerism asserts an evident link between objectification and the commodity, just as porn's profits undoubtedly allow Treehorn to indulge in his lust for stuff, and beer ads seem unimaginable without scantily clad young women. Underwriting his expostulation is the much-remarked-upon, though rarely fully articulated, familial likeness of sexual fetishism and commodity fetishism.[9]

Yet neither of these responses goes far enough, even if it still seems necessary to keep in mind these manifest ties between the commodification of women and the sexualizing of the commodity. One problem with both commodity fetishism and sexual fetishism is that neither is regarded as a problem anymore. On the one hand, in the West, late capitalism's saturation of both public and psychic space seems a *fait accompli*, lending to the commodity form the spurious dignity of an epistemology—now we can only know objects as commodities. But attendant on reduction of the object-world to the commodity form must surely be the sense in which in a sexual register, fetishism has been transformed into something more akin to an anodyne "lifestyle choice," precisely because of such a designation's amenability to recuperation under capitalism. Fetishism ends because it is now *sold*, largely immune to moralizing judgments concerning the "proper" and normative but also, worryingly perhaps, more than ever before an essential and structural part of a matrix that includes the psychic and the economic.[10] Sexual fetishism now becomes indistinguishable from commodity fetishism, with both seemingly irrelevant to a celebratory consumer culture, in which even our kinks can be sold back to us for a profit—which should compel us to wonder if those kinks are indeed really ours.[11] But there is no going back.[12]

This problem is all at once a problem of the subject, the social, the economic, and the theoretical. The difficulty has to do with mediation and is at least as old as Freud: how can we coordinate the public and the private, the social and the psychic? As Fredric Jameson points out, Freud introduces this particular problematic as early as "Creative Writers and Daydreaming," in which our individual revulsion at the fantasies and wish fulfillments of others is overcome by the purely formal pleasures of the work of art (Jameson 1988). Whatever the inarguable benefits of such an approach—and Jameson details many of them, tracing the histories of several crucial Freudian-Marxist syntheses from the Frankfurt School to Sartre—they proceed, as it were, from the inside out, a trajectory that appears unusable for an understanding of the waning of distance between commodity fetishism and sexual fetishism. In contrast to Freud's conception of the work of art, the commodity form as well as the fetish object comes to structure the psyche and even perhaps the social from without. Yet both are seemingly characterized by the ease with which they move back and forth, from shop window to unconscious and back again. In this sense, too, the fetish object now seems to come to us domesticated and anodyne, including its own interpretation like the instructions that come with Ikea furniture.

Similarly for Adorno, for whom Freud's insights play a crucial role, the subject as such must be revealed as a historical category and construction, not as an ontological starting point for thought. Thus the ego—its attenuation under the Culture Industry and fascism alike—is social and historical through and through; and it is to the id, the libido, and the unconscious that Adorno looks to find what might be presocial in the subject, the very libido that has come to be colonized by the commodity form. But to the extent that the dialectic of enlightenment binds together self-preservation and self-destruction in a false reconciliation of ego and id, it is not only that analytic therapy cannot alleviate the subject's symptoms but also that this problem is broadly social: self-preservation, in principle motivated to keep the subject safe from a threatening nature, regresses into self-destruction, the repression of human nature, that at the far end takes the name of Auschwitz. Nothing like a positive integration of the subject is possible—and here Adorno shares with Lacan an extreme allergy to ego psychology—and even the category of sublimation ultimately seems only affirmative of the prevailing social and economic order.[13] If, as my polemical head-note suggests, "[i]n psycho-analysis nothing is true except the exaggerations" (Adorno 1974, 49), this is because for Adorno the insights of Freud function best when extrapolated fully in the social sphere, which in this historical moment has irrevocably reduced the subject. To put it slightly differently, for Freud the psyche's aim—maturity—is dialectically related for Adorno to history's own very troubled path to maturity, the Enlightenment itself, for which the psyche is subject but mostly object, and what was promised as the release from our self-incurred tutelage has twisted into self-domination. But it is here, too, that his reflections on art's impossible autonomy as well as on the primacy of the object that open other possibilities for the subject: "The core of individuality would be comparable to those utterly individuated works of art which spurn all schemata and whose analysis will rediscover universal moments in their extreme individuation—a participation in a typicality that is hidden from the participants themselves" (Adorno 1973, 162, qtd. in Whitebook 59). In this profoundly Hegelian moment the distinction between part and whole, subject and object, falls away, or almost; and were it possible to pare away the need for self-preservation (and the attenuation of this principle is a precondition for a nonsubsumptive relation to the object), it would be possible to discern a true freedom, which otherwise can only be imagined for us in art, and there typically only negatively.[14]

The Big Lebowski reworks this logic. Whatever else it may be about, it takes as its subjects castration and exchange and thus the fetish, in many of its forms; and so the fetish will be for us as it is for it a privileged figure that can uncannily move between the registers of psychic and social. This movement takes several forms. Perhaps the film's most obvious debt to Hawks's *The Big Sleep* (1946) occurs on the level of plot: here, as in its canonical antecedent, events follow each other with a logic verging on the aleatory.[15] Indeed, *The Big Lebowski* begins to undermine narrative as a way to frustrate the structure of exchange as such, as the plot spirals deliriously through a virtual anthology of incomplete exchanges on both the macro and micro levels.[16] Thus the lack of commensurability between and among episodes on a narrative level does not necessarily entail their persistence as free-floating and exchangeable monads but rather seems to assert their critical irreducibility, a willful intent not to be subsumed in a narrative whole. Bunny Lebowski (Tara Reid), the putative kidnapping victim to be ransomed by her husband, the Big Lebowski (David Huddleston), cannot be ransomed or bought back because, as we come to understand, she was never kidnapped to begin with, and so she cannot be subject to exchange in that sense. Nor is she even Bunny Lebowski to begin with, as we discover that her real name is Fawn Gunderson. And the ransom itself, as the capital necessary for this exchange for a woman who is not missing, proves to be a ringer for a ringer: the Dude's friend Walter (John Goodman) substitutes a bag full of his underwear for the original briefcase, which we discover proves not to have had the money in it either. But if Bunny cannot be bought on the diegetic level—made an object to circulate according to the vagaries of exchange—this does not prevent the camera from fetishizing her, framing her as the object of its (and our) voyeuristic and indeed fetishistic gaze.[17] The film's allusion to Kubrick's *Lolita* (1962) is pertinent here: as Bunny paints her toenails she propositions the Dude, "I'll suck your cock for $1000," immediately adding "Brandt can't watch, though, or he has to pay a hundred."[18] He responds, "I'm just gonna find a cash machine." Evidently Bunny can easily fix both the Dude and Brandt's (Phillip Seymour Hoffman) desires: the first for exchange (both economic and erotic), the second for a fetishistic and voyeuristic pleasure. But how distinct, finally, are these? The frustration of the former means that we as viewers have recourse only to the latter.

Yet like all the other exchanges and transactions in which the Dude is involved, this one will remain necessarily incomplete. Indeed, the only exchange the Dude successfully executes opens the film, rather than providing a more typical narrative conclusion: he writes a check for a quart of cream (presumably for his White Russians). Subjective desire is framed in terms of economic exchange here with Bunny, even as the Dude is shown to lack the means—capital—for exchange as such. After a lingering close-up of her painted toenails, the camera zooms out to reveal Bunny in her bikini, with the camera replicating the fetishist's logic of the part standing in for the whole. Bunny, however, looks at the camera and therefore at the audience over her sunglasses, as if to reverse the trajectory of the fetishist's gaze. She will consent to being a fetish object only according to the tenets of another, more material economy, and at this point a properly psychoanalytic surplus enjoyment shades into a so-called surplus value. Her big toe, the metonymic fetish object, will then reappear in ways that she will not: first as seemingly severed from the foot, both a contingent object and also a putative guarantee of her physical presence as captive, and then later still attached to her foot as it depresses the gas pedal of her Porsche. Intact, it gives the lie at once to the claims of the kidnappers who sent the severed toe and more generally to the logic of fetishism as such. If in the first case the toe is detached by the camera to promote erotic and fetishistic desire and later to reveal the violence and power that underwrite them when the toe is actually severed, Bunny's direct gaze revokes the first, while the instabilities and exigencies of economic exchange are condemned along with the latter. The real toe, cut from the foot of a nihilist's girlfriend, is then paradoxically enough so far from "the toe's" initial introduction and reference that its ultimate relation to a particular and real body seems negligible—or rather in its promotion as irreducibly particular it nonetheless enters into the circulation of exchange, in which its identity, its particularity, dissolves. For the pervert (or film viewer), the fetish may be contingent, but it is absolutely particular even as it stands in for the maternal phallus—without it the sexual act is impossible. But transformed into a commodity and compelled to submit to exchange its particularity dissolves—"I can get you a toe," says Walter, suggesting that the logic of exchange has already impinged upon the particularity of the fetish object. In seeking to sever the toe, to put it in play in a system of erotic and economic exchange, the film rehearses a whole series of unstable and unrealizable exchanges for which this is a model: the toe is real; it guarantees presence and identity; it solicits desire; it circulates and prompts exchange, undoing identity; the toe is fake; there is no exchange.

The German nihilists confront the Dude himself with a similar dilemma: "Give us the money, Lebowski, or we cut off your Johnson!" Is this not an injunction to be a fetishist? To acknowledge the role of money, exchange, as fictitious and as necessary as the maternal phallus—or experience real castration?[19] Your money or your life; *le père ou pire*. The Dude has no money and seems attached to his Johnson, but at the risk of losing the latter he must pursue or at least acknowledge the former, especially insofar as it now has been explicitly linked to castration and lack, which is to say, exchange and his Johnson. The fetish is an Imaginary substitute for a real phallus—thus, at least in terms of the nihilists' threat, money exceeds its purely Symbolic function and gets caught up in anxiety about loss, castration, and desire.[20] That the Dude's Johnson can be linked with economic exchange at all must attest then not only to the libidinization of money and capital, its promotion to a fetish that covers over a lack but also to the economic aspect of the fetish itself.

Whatever the Dude's problems, we cannot diagnose him as a sexual fetishist, despite his evident attraction to Bunny and her toe and to his Johnson, if not to money. Indeed, the film's central fantasy sequence, *Gutterballs*, a pastiche of Busby Berkeley's dance numbers, seems at first to depend on a fetishistic objectification of women's bodies before modulating into something else. Berkeley made his reputation by providing Depression-era audiences with spectacle, combining choreography of military precision with lavish

Figure 4.1 *Gutterballs*

sets and provocative costumes. Berkeley's success hinged on his conflation of voyeuristic fantasy, technological spectacle, and visual excess. The identically clad young women that constitute the Berkeley spectacle are framed for the viewer not according to the logic of montage but rather by the moving camera—it has often been observed that in his production numbers the camera dances more than the dancers.[21] On a formal level this single perspective authorizes and promotes a voyeuristic position for the spectator, one that is sealed by the costumes and the iconography of the spectacle itself. As Mulvey puts it, "Woman as erotic object is the leitmotif of erotic spectacle: from the pinups to striptease, from Ziegfeld to Busby Berkeley, she holds the look, plays to and signifies male desire" (2004 841). Yet as this is the Dude's fantasy, it seems worthwhile pointing out the extent to which he can avoid the division between fetishistic scopophilia and voyeurism that Mulvey describes: he himself is the bearer of a very particular look.[22] The Dude, drugged by Jackie Treehorn (Ben Gazzara), slips into his dream sequence (from which wish fulfillment is certainly not absent), which condenses a number of key elements from the narrative: he himself is dressed as the cable repairman from Bunny Lebowski's porno video *Logjammin'* that Maude Lebowski (Julianne Moore), feminist artist and the Big Lebowski's daughter (and hence Bunny's stepdaughter), had played for him earlier. Maude affirms her associations with high culture in a pseudo-Wagnerian costume, complete with horned helmet and trident. It is hard to resist seeing these accessories as evidence of her phallic power; and far from being merely erotic objects, the women of the chorus come to us decorated with phallic bowling pins, whose own iconic status has already been evoked by the dream's pornographic title sequence of a pin sliding between two very breast-like bowling balls. The sheer plethora of phallic signifiers at play here undermine the status of the phallus and fetish both, now no longer single but multiple, and with it any suggestion that the Dude himself is a fetishist in that older sense—no mere fantasy of a phallic woman here but rather the inflation and multiplication of the phallus to undo its fetishistic specificity. For although he evidently derives satisfaction from this fantasy, it cannot be said that he has at last found that lost object that was never lost because it never existed: the maternal phallus. That impossible phallus is everywhere—except where it should be. If the fetish functions as a veil, covering over the traumatic sight of absence, the Dude chooses to confront that absence in this fantasy sequence. The beatific smile on his face as he passes like a bowling ball between the legs of the women who straddle the alley is decidedly not that of one who has disavowed castration.

This fantasy, both in its condensation of elements from elsewhere in the film and in its tendential approach to autonomy—complete as it is with its own title sequence—invites its own aesthetic parsing as well, especially since such considerations have already been tabled by no less than Jackie Treehorn himself:

> THE DUDE. How's the smut business, Jackie?
> TREEHORN. I wouldn't know, Dude. I deal in publishing, entertainment, political advocacy, and—
> THE DUDE. Which one was *Logjammin'*?
> TREEHORN. Regrettably, it's true, standards have fallen in adult entertainment. It's video, Dude. Now that we're competing with the amateurs, we can't afford to invest that little extra in story, production value, feeling. [He taps his forehead with one finger.] People forget that the brain is the biggest erogenous zone—
> THE DUDE. On you, maybe.

Prior to this, during the abbreviated screening of *Logjammin'*, Maude, artist that she is, permits herself an aesthetic judgment on the video—"The story is ludicrous"—which comes to inform the Dude's question but also raises a whole range of aesthetic questions we might have felt to be irrelevant to the consumption of pornography. To begin, it aligns Maude with Treehorn, both of whom maintain that a modicum of narrative is essential to porn, as if it required the legitimation of aesthetics—as if, as in Adorno, what once was art suffers from the pressures of commodification. Treehorn's answer

Figure 4.2   The Dude enjoying his fantasy

unsurprisingly points to the necessity of economic rationalization, brought on by competition from other media,
and what must be rationalized out of the picture are "story,
production value, feeling," whose loss reveals pornography
as the instrumental object it seems always to have been,
particularly insofar as this loss precludes the imaginative
participation of the viewing subject. But the Dude's witty
reply to Treehorn's bad faith gives lie to *Gutterballs* itself,
which, presumably, his own psyche offers up as an aesthetic
remediation of everything deficient in *Logjammin'*—that
is, *Gutterballs*, spectacle on an operatic scale, meticulously,
obsessively, includes and foregrounds all the artistic qualities
and aims thought lacking in its instrumental counterpart.
The Wagnerian motifs virtually guarantee *Gutterballs*'s aspi-
ration to offer a *Gesamtkunstwerk*, including performance,
song, architecture, dance, and bowling to affirm its totalizing ambitions and to provide "story, production value,
feeling" for its audience, which presumably is now no longer the solitary consumer of pornography—the sexual act is
conspicuous in its absence—but rather the collective audience of the larger film itself.

We cannot then dismiss *Gutterballs* as mere parody or irony, as its totalizing ambit comes virtually to characterize the film as a whole, as it omnivorously evokes and explores other aesthetic modes and forms, high and low, including them within its own frame. Thus the film gives us Maude, painter of "strongly vaginal" works; Knox Harrington (David Thewlis), video artist; the Dude's landlord Marty (Jack Kehler), a dancer and performance artist who invites the Dude to see his "cycle"; Arthur Digby Sellers (Harry Bugin), writer for the television series *Branded*; the German nihilists, who formerly recorded as Autobahn; and even at the limit Treehorn himself. It bears repeating that such extensive citation of other aesthetic forms within film betrays in advance its own self-promotion as the ultimate realization of these others' particular means and ends, even film's self-satisfied triumph in a game it has rigged in advance;[23] but in an immanent sense, each of these examples comes to invite comment and judgment from audiences both within and without the film. Maude's paintings, then, strongly linked in both their production and content to her body—"Does the female form make you uncomfortable, Mr. Lebowski?"—meet with the Dude's puzzled approval, and this despite their experimental basis and her challenging mien. Alternately, no example of Knox Harrington's video art is available to the Dude or to us—which in the end seems not to matter, given how the film is at pains to present this character as unlikable. Marty's dance quintet, performed to Mussorgsky's *Pictures at an Exhibition*, likewise meets with the benign approval of the Dude, Donny, and Walter and aspires, like the film itself, to integrate diverse forms—dance, music, art—within a single work. We might even wish to measure its success by the extent to which it invites neither profanity nor violence from Walter. Of course Walter prefers *Branded*, standing in awe of its writer of 156 episodes, Arthur Digby Sellers, who is enclosed in an iron lung and is now fully as technologically mediated as his series, if not literally a testament to Barthes's "The Death of the Author." The electronic rhythms of Autobahn contrast sharply with the Dude's preference for Creedence Clearwater Revival, and their album

Nagelbett, featuring "Violate U Blue" and "Take It In," fully anticipate Jackie Treehorn's posthuman future of "interactive erotic software," rendering sex "100 percent electronic." The oppositions that govern these examples tell us much, arguing that however puzzling, awkward, impenetrable, or enigmatic contemporary art can be—feminist action painting, modern dance—it is to be preferred to the electronic, the simulacral, the prosthetic, the technologically reproduced, electro-pop, video art, and network television alike, which everywhere come to stand for what is inauthentic and deleterious about the culture of this world. This film signals its allegiance with art.

Like the enclosing tendencies noted earlier, in one sense we cannot be surprised that here film as a medium seeks to distinguish itself from smaller screens, its competitors the television and computer monitor, each of which summoned to bear the opprobrium of its analog ancestor. Yet in another sense, what both of these tendencies—film as the ultimate art; film as distinct from video—come to question is the essence of film itself. Not for *The Big Lebowski* a notional "purity": little enough here intimates film as a monad, an in-itself—quite the opposite, as these citations of other media as well as the film's own references to the Western, film noir, the musical, and other genres all imply a rich mediation at work. That is, if essence there is here, it is necessarily impure, heterogeneous; and yet it seems still a question. In a late essay, "Art and the Arts," Adorno comes to reflect on the fraying of the individual arts, their restless blending into one another in a bewildering variety of manners that come to express new possibilities but also new problems for the idea of art itself. He writes, "The negativity of the concept of art impinges on its contents. Its own nature, not the impotence of our thoughts about it, forbids us to define it; its innermost principle, that of utopia, rebels against the domination of nature that its definition implies" (Adorno 2003, 386). So far, so good: art's own concept is negative; it must be so to resist its wholesale liquidation as and through the concept in order to hold to a utopian future in which conceptual—but not solely conceptual—domination is absent. "It does not wish to remain what it once was" (386), lest it be caught by the concept. But now Adorno's thought will itself shift and provide a startlingly new constellation: "The question whether film is art or not is idle. On the one hand, as Benjamin was first to show in his essay 'The Work of Art in the Age of Mechanical Reproduction,' film comes closest to its own essence where it ruthlessly eliminates the attribute of aura that characterized all art before film, the illusion of transcendence guaranteed by its context—to put it another way, where film renounces symbolic and other elements that confer meaning to a degree that could scarcely be imagined by realist painting and literature" (Adorno 2003, 386). We have already considered in some detail the products of the Culture Industry, and film particularly, as too affirmative, too tied to the world as it is for all the wrong reasons; and we have also considered a number of Adorno's responses to Benjamin and mechanical reproduction. How could it be that film's indexicality, now via Benjamin opposed to illusory transcendence, can come to be validated in and as art? How is it now that film can be elevated to art—and less pressingly, how does the question of film as art come now to be "idle"? Dialectically.

First, the ambivalent validation of painting and dance alike hinges upon a tension the film is keen to exploit: unlike more technologically mediated forms, these both evince a relation to particular subjects and particular bodies in ways that earn the film's approval as expressive and enigmatic objects themselves. And yet in both, aura seems intact, ritual and distance maintained, as even Walter dons a suit and tie for Marty's performance at Crane Jackson's Fountain Street Theater, and Maude's paintings, little seen by either the Dude or us, remain remote, especially in comparison to film. But if this is so, and film approaches art in its rejection not only of aura but also of "symbolic and other elements"—style? "story, production values, feelings"?—then in the film's own terms it veers dangerously close to porn itself, *Logjammin'* rather than *Gutterballs*, video and the instrumental commodity rather than a total work that includes lack. Second, it would certainly be idle to celebrate Adorno's dropping of the other dialectical shoe, a wholesale revision of the Culture Industry thesis, and the longed for articulation of what film might be beyond a ceaseless domination of the subject. This is not that. In the context of "The Culture Industry" section of the *Dialectic of Enlightenment*, what fully earns film, radio, and others besides all the excoriation Adorno can muster, is, finally, less their offences against art (although those, too) than the extent to which they come to take their role in the domination of the subject, insisting, within a remorseless mechanical monotony that finally the subject can only be a passive thing.[24] Thus painting and dance retain their ties to the expressive subject and illusory aura both, while film then seeks less their expressive power than a way of conferring meaning and rejecting domination that would distinguish it from its contemporaries, video, television, and computer.

For Adorno this might be accomplished through another turn of the dialectical screw:

> For all its abstinence from aura and subjective intention, film technique inevitably feeds elements of meaning into the final product: through the script, the photographed images, the camera's point of view, the cutting—methods not unlike those adopted in music or painting, which also want the material to appear naked before the viewer or listener but inevitably preform it in the process. Although film would like to discard its artlike qualities while adhering to the intrinsic laws governing it as a form—almost as if art were in conflict with its own artistic principle—film remains art in its rebellion and even enlarges art. (Adorno 2003, 386)

Film finds its art in a seemingly antiartistic eschewal of expression and intention, by which it is hoped the objects of the world might finally be offered up to speak as if for themselves. It is an impossibility finally and yet nonetheless an impossibility that enlarges art: not through a cannibalization of older forms, nor through an unstable distinction between film and other technologically reproducible media, but through its rebellion against style, mediation, and expression themselves as they have come to be given historically, a rebellion that it is hoped might make expression, desire, an apprehension of the world possible again.

We are now a very long way from *Gutterballs* indeed, whose own agenda cannot be squared with this one without interpretive violence. On one hand its allegiance to an ideal of film, though an impure one, sides it and the larger film of which it is a part with fantasy and the subject, whose pleasures, bodily or aesthetic, it solicits to attest to its success. But this impurity must be given its proper name—contradiction— and so prompt further thought. For *Gutterballs* distinguishes itself further from *Logjammin'* in that it is not for sale or exchange but is rather (diegetically at least) a private fantasy of the Dude's that the larger narrative frame pretends merely to present unadorned. Of course the sequence's intense stylization and spectacle make it seem anything but the objective record of private fantasy; and yet insofar as it is fantasy, whether the Dude's or the film's own—and a fantasy that has a totalizing reach, expanding via its inclusion of so many other aesthetic forms and even representing (via bowling!) an image of woman and man as reconciled—it seems a fantasy of a better world, of utopia. Such an image cannot be maintained—even in fantasy—and the nihilists return with their castrating scissors, shortly to be replaced, with a shift of diegetic gears, by the police who pick up the drugged Dude stumbling along the highway. Belief in a better world opposes belief in nothing; utopian fantasy stands opposed to the oppressive social world. But whatever is utopian about this sequence depends on the extent to which it is at least putatively private, the spectacular mise-en-scène then to be registered as an admission of the impossibility of giving "objective" body and image to such a private wish, to such an in-itself, without giving it style, without inevitably distorting it or preforming it, and without offering it up for sale— which finally then comes to be at one with the *bilderverbot* and the prohibition on representations of utopia itself. For *The Big Lebowski*, then, fantasy itself must be accorded all the ontological dignity of the other objects of the world, its reality also registered as best the medium can—finally as more real than the false world that opposes it.

Here at least, then, fantasy—and especially utopian fantasy—shares with the object the danger of coming to be dominated and transformed into an object for sale, its particularity obviated and contained. But if this is so, if private fantasy and material object alike constitute the raw material of the film with both at risk of being commodified and transformed into their opposites, then the film's own strategy must shift, and its obsessive concern with non sequiturs and mistaken identity, failed ransoms and doubly fake ringers, erotic and economic exchange, and both commodity and sexual fetishism appears as a willful agenda to frustrate exchange as such, a determined and pervasive short-circuiting of identity thinking in many of its forms, such that some sort of particularity, both subjective and objective, might come to be discerned.

Of course the film offers a material and objective counterpart to the Dude's operatic porno fantasy, one whose particularity is equally complex, impure, and heterogeneous. Over and over again, he and his friends dwell on the rug urinated upon by the thugs sent to collect a debt that is not his: "The rug really tied the room together, man" is his own succinct formulation. In strictly narrative terms, the loss of the rug inspires the Dude to seek out the Big Lebowski, and in material terms the Dude celebrates its particularity while the thugs violate and reduce it. But the rug possesses a crucial subjective and psychic dimension, too—indeed, it is the film's privileged object insofar as it binds together the material and psychic, the objective and the subjective. It is, to start, a fetish: not, as in a crude Freudianism, a substitute for and a reminder of the mother's genitals (even if Maude comes to be identified with it) but rather a privileged object for its spatial function, how it organizes (domestic, if not bourgeois) space in a structured and artful way that comes to seem analogous to film itself. It is not a veil that covers a traumatic absence but, like film, a screen or matrix onto which a very particular fantasy will be projected. That fantasy certainly includes the threat of absence, of failed pleasure and dissatisfaction (as the Dude never does get his rug back), but it also refuses to be reduced to the fetishistic play of presence and absence that for the apparatus theorists governs our experience of film. In his first dream sequence the Dude witnesses the rug flying over Los Angeles,[25] displaying a spatial power that trumps any libidinal charge it might possess. In both the dream and the film the rug bears the weight of a repressed utopian agenda for art, which here entails a desire for the transcendence of the city and the material world, the obverse and extension of its decorative function. But the Dude's bowling ball brings him back down to earth—the material world will not be sublated by sheer fantasy, especially since that utopian desire seems to have abandoned Left politics as such, as the Dude's own memories of 1960s student radicalism are represented as private nostalgia at best. In this present world, where millionaire pornographer Jackie Treehorn is uncritically granted status in the community that the Dude disrupts and where porn itself seems virtually an epistemology, finding itself prefixed with *lifestyle* and even—or especially—*commodity*, then we should note again the extent to which even sexual pathologies such as fetishism have also been motivated to serve a capital from which they were once, presumably, distinct. Herbert Marcuse's notion of repressive desublimation is relevant here, as what Žižek would refer to as the contemporary superego's injunction to enjoy serves the individual less than it serves consumer society and corporate capital.[26]

What all descriptions and definitions of the fetish share is the ascription of a scandalously "improper" value to an object—an idol, a commodity, or a spike heel—the elevation of a contingent object to an overdetermined place in the structure. And while we can point to the uncanny and disturbing effects of such an elevation, whether they be blasphemous, materialistic, or pathological/symptomatic, we should also note how structures of belief, exchange, and sexual relation all seem to require this contingent object. No economy of belief, exchange, or sexuality can ever consolidate itself without the contingent object, which thus shares something with Derrida's supplement or Lacan's *objet petit a* above and beyond its ideological or symptomatic description—beyond, even, the minimal utopian function already evoked. But then from the perspective Adorno supplies us with, the object as such can

Figure 4.3   Maude and the rug over Los Angeles

never be anything but this—always excessive, always, finally, beyond language and thought—and so the object is *always* a fetish, or at least always seems so from our perspective within economies of language, thought, and exchange, with fetishism now (potentially at least) no longer a pathology but an attempt and failure to grasp the object's elusive noumenal being and particularity. It is not that the object is excessive and scandalous but rather that thought and language are limits, limits we are too often satisfied to remain within, as if our thinking, too, like the Dude's, "had become uptight." From this perspective all kinds of monolithic identities and ideologies begin to break down, revealing their own contingency, inviting utopian alternatives.[27]

The reason for this is material. The fetish, in Marx's conception, argues for an important link between the registers of the material, the individual, and even the spiritual. Marx writes, "If commodities could speak, they would say this: our use value may interest men, but it does not belong to us as objects. What does belong to us as objects, however, is our value. Our own intercourse as commodities proves it" (1976, 176–77). The eclipse of use value by exchange value under capitalism lends commodities an uncanny life. For Marx, the fetish is an index not of our materialism but rather of the extent to which we are *not materialistic enough*: we insist on attributing to the commodity a "mystical character," "metaphysical subtleties," and "theological niceties" (Marx 1976, 163). Commodity fetishism testifies to Enlightenment's becoming myth: just as for Adorno an "excess" of rationality leads to irrationality, here an "excess" of materialism entails the return of spirit and spirits—not the gods of so-called primitive peoples, but now the full fluorescence of the libidinal and the metaphysical in the service of the economic.[28]

Yet the "metaphysical subtleties" that come to characterize the commodity form necessarily get attached to the work of art, too—as I have discussed in the context of *Repo Man*, "The absolute artwork coincides with the absolute commodity" (Adorno 1997, 21)—and with those subtleties come the alignment if not identity of the fetish and the work of art itself. What such an alignment tells us, though, will add further dimensions to both of our previous construals of fetishism in its psychic and material aspects. If it is indeed the case that we are not materialistic enough and so find ourselves compelled to impute a specious ideality onto the alluring commodity, then with the most minimal shift in perspective that "false" ideality coincides with what is most necessary and distinctive about the work of art: "If in monopoly capitalism it is primarily exchange value, not use value, which is consumed, in the modern artwork it is its abstractness, that irritating indeterminateness of what it is and to what purpose it is, that becomes the cipher of what the work is . . . [I]t is a provocation, it challenges the illusion that life goes on, and at the same time it is a means for that aesthetic distancing that traditional fantasy no longer achieves" (Adorno 1997, 21–22). The work of art translates the aura of the commodity form into an enigma, even into a kind of frustration, a maddening puzzle that abjures easy consumption and so attempts to threaten the endless process of consumption as a whole, with its claim that that is all there is and that to live is to consume. It seeks to transform those "metaphysical subtleties" and "theological niceties" back into what they always were: contradictions. And in its cipher-like character it achieves what fantasy— wish fulfillment—cannot: offering up an image that cannot be easily exchanged, one that thus aims at a particularity and objectivity beyond the private and subjective. While the operatic aspects of *Gutterballs* and the domestic qualities of the rug possess little enough of the opacity or enigmatical *en-soi* of a Beckett or Schoenberg, the modernist paragons Adorno implicitly gestures toward here, they nonetheless work toward a tendential autonomy beyond their function, raising questions and resisting answers. Beyond their fetish function, their gratuitousness and specificity always inti- mate that they are more than they appear.

Yet it may be, despite the aesthetic agenda I have tried to discern in *Gutterballs* and the rug, that, finally, they hew too closely to the commodity form to be able to imply a cancellation of that form—as if, finally, art could effect such a change. Or, to put it another way, it may be that whatever aesthetic qualities or agenda these things might be thought to possess can only be supplemental, mere culinary embel- lishments that, far from contributing to their autonomy, finally only confirm them only as decorous commodities themselves. But to conclude this would be to miss that they are necessarily social, too, despite their ties to private fan- tasy and domestic space, and that their trajectory toward reconciliation and utopia is made necessary by a society and economy that would have them be not themselves, neither art nor objects but fetishes and nothing more. Or again, to put in the terms already evoked in my consideration of *Repo Man*, art must "metamorphose into a thing in order to break the catastrophic spell of things" (Adorno 1967c, 233). We might come to see, then, the origins of these works of art in the commodity—an origin and affinity foisted upon them by society—as an essential step in breaking the spell.

> But the guilt [artworks] bear of fetishism does not disqualify art, any more so than it disqualifies anything culpable; for in the universally, socially mediated world nothing stands external to its nexus of guilt. The truth content of artworks, which is indeed

their social truth, is predicated on their fetish character. The principle of heteronomy, apparently the counterpart of fetishism, is the principle of exchange, and in it domination is masked. Only what does not submit to that principle acts as the plenipotentiary of what is free from domination; only what is useless can stand in for the stunted use value. Artworks are plenipotentiaries of things that are no longer distorted by exchange, profit, and the false needs of a degraded humanity. (Adorno 1997, 227)

Dialectically then, fetishism at once is false, in need of unmasking, a source of guilt for the work of art and society both, and also a "pathology" that suggests a value beyond exchange and a need that may seem pathological and as false as the spurious need for the commodity. To put it the other way round, the work of art's illusory autonomy, its implied value beyond exchange, renders it a fetish, with fetishism then, like dialectics, becoming the right thought for the wrong world—that is, a distorted desire for singularity, particularity, and even, finally, subjectivity and distorted because there is no context available in which such a desire could be better realized or articulated.

Indeed, the identification of the fetish with not only psychic and material economies but also the work of art itself provides a suitable expansion of our contexts so far. *The Big Lebowski* is a cult film: initially a disappointment at the box office, it found its audience via home video, coming ultimately to spawn an almost endless number of websites with accompanying merchandise as well as several annual Lebowski Fests, typically featuring not only a screening of the film but also, of course, bowling. While an extensive discussion of the cultic dimensions of the film would lead us too far afield, at least two points merit mentioning: first, its status as a cult object cannot be uncritically celebrated, as if its popularity somehow rendered it more authentic and isolated it from its status as a commodity film. Barbara Klinger puts it this way: "Given the aftermarket's vitality, the contemporary Hollywood cult film is not a thing apart. Certain species of cult cinema are not discontinuous from dominant industry or social practices; instead they represent continuity with, even a shining realization of, the dynamics of media circulation today. In this sense, cult is a logical extension of replay culture: it achieves the kind of penetration into viewers' 'hearts and minds' that media convergence and multi-windowed distribution promote; cultish viewing, in turn, represents a particularly dedicated and insistent pursuit of media inspired by replay" (Klinger 2010, 6). Less asserting the exceptional status of the film and how it differs from other Hollywood products, its veneration as a cultic object stands as an emblematic instantiation of commodity culture as second nature, internalized and endlessly reiterable.

And yet second, as we considered in the context of *The Maltese Falcon*, the work of art still bears within itself its origins in magic and ritual, origins that betray its status as cult or fetish object. Indeed, a work's fetish character—its irreducible particularity, its yearned-for autonomy—holds as its secret not only the desire to frustrate exchange but also and fundamentally the aim of providing another form of rationality. It is akin to the cultic object insofar as both attempt to pry open a space for a nonconceptual, nondominating mimesis of nature; but where the cultic object is prehistorical, the work of art is historically and socially mediated, and what appears least rational and most fetishistic about it—its cipher-like quality, its enigmatic being—should come to seem instead a constellated form of an expanded notion of reason itself, one that abjures the violence inherent in conceptual thought as it now stands and one that holds fast to the possibility that reason could be other than it is, with the possibility of new relations to nature and to others. If under high bourgeois society, art's illusory or fetishistic aspects required the demystification of ideological critique, now, from the heyday of modernism to our contemporary moment, the ubiquity of the commodity form has rendered the illusory real, and it is precisely that spurious reality that the involuted work of art seeks to negate.

This has also to do with how fetishism as such has always depended upon charging the fetishist as "primitive"—whether, as William Pietz, Homi Bhabha, and others have pointed out,[29] in a terrain determined by a then-nascent colonialism or in an orthodox Freudianism, in a matrix that positions the fetishist as immature and infantile because of his disavowal of castration. While the former case depends on the geopolitical, social, and economic determinants of exploitation and enforced "uneven development," the latter presents itself as a diagnosis proper. Both descriptions depend on a position of superiority or even mastery above and apart from the pathologized fetishist, whether this latter is conceived as the African worshipping an idol, the pervert with his spike heel, or the consumer in front of the shop window. While it would certainly be useful and instructive to submit such hierarchies to an obvious but still pertinent deconstruction, it might be more revealing to construe them as articulating something like an elementary history of modernity itself— the dialectic of enlightenment—with the worship of the fetish telling us less, perhaps, about the fetishist, and more about the modern cultural analyst, who, by virtue of taking a privileged position above the phenomenon of the fetish, stands in a position cleared for her or him by an imperialist and class-bound modernity. The modern itself depends on an othering of the "primitive" and the perverse; but also, perhaps, to the extent to which modernity depends on an analogous division along the lines of class, the scandalous other term that holds the same position in the West as so-called "primitive" societies did under imperialisms of various sorts. Indeed, we may go so far as to argue that the *point du capiton* that binds together commodity and sexual fetishism is a conception of class itself, which irritates precisely because at this historical stage of global capitalism class is no longer supposed to exist in the West. Yet exist it does: the Dude's inversion of categories—the commodification of women's bodies and commodity fetishism—depends on his own marginal class status, in the same way that fetishism as such has always depended on a conception of the modern and modernization as uneven and as classed.

Class is a subterranean theme in *The Big Lebowski* and perhaps nowhere more evident than at the end of the Dude's initial encounter with his namesake:

THE BIG LEBOWSKI. Your revolution is over, Mr. Lebowski. Condolences. The bums lost. My advice is to do what

your parents did; get a job, sir. The bums will always lose!
Do you hear me, Lebowski?
[The Dude walks out and shuts the door]
THE BIG LEBOWSKI. The bums will always lose!
BRANDT. How was your meeting, Mr. Lebowski?
THE DUDE. Okay. The old man told me to take any rug in
the house.

Here the long death of the 1960s continues, with the Big
Lebowski reveling in the extinction of various utopian
impulses and agents, now reduced under capitalism to
so many "bums." But two important facts are notewor-
thy: most immediately, one bum wins, as the Dude exits
with the rug for which he has come, if not *the* rug, which,
like the work of art here, remains elusive when not soiled
and discredited; and in any event Maude will come to
claim this rug as hers, as it was not the Big Lebowski's
to give. And second, the Dude is surely a bum in some
sense despite his revolutionary past as author of the Port
Huron Statement;[30] for one of the mysteries the film leaves
us with, another puzzle and problem for the principle of
exchange, is precisely what he does to support his bowling and White Russian habits—"Are you employed, sir?"
the Big Lebowski asks with evident contempt. But here
again the promise of utopia pushes forward some tentative
shoots, for if the Dude does not work, then he cannot be
said to be alienated by that work; and while he is part of
the unemployed and underemployed structurally necessary
for capitalism to function, his history of 1960s radicalism makes it equally possible to see in his unemployment
a keeping-faith with that great situationist injunction
"Never work!" As Fredric Jameson asks, "Yet was it not the
whole purpose of the great socialist movements precisely
to get rid of labor in the first place? . . . [A]nd have not the
most consequent contemporary socialist theoreticians con-
templated at some length the ambivalence of the 'jobless
future' which is both a nightmare and a *promesse du bonheur*' all at once" (Jameson 2005, 150). Indeed, the Dude's
participation in the economy and the Symbolic as such is
curiously liminal, announced by his lack of identification:

all he has in his wallet is a card allowing him to write checks at the grocery store. The Dude and his friends and bowling partners, Walter and Donny, form something like a minimal anthology of 1960s male types, with the Dude as the pot-fuelled former radical, Walter as the traumatized Vietnam veteran, and Donny as the surfer.[31] With these characters the film meditates on the fate of the 1960s, its various types, and its revolutionary and utopian aspirations: the Dude has seemingly retreated into pot and bowling, while Walter continues to relive the Vietnam War in a pathological though not entirely convincing fashion, and Donny is reduced to an impoverished repertoire of empty non sequiturs.

But the Big Lebowski and Treehorn are historical figures, too, though structurally opposed along the lines of history and class. The Big Lebowski's house, for example, done up as an ancestral manor, asserts a triumphal stranglehold on history itself as the history of the victorious class, the 1 percent—and this despite the fact that he is really nouveau riche, having married into wealth. It stands in sharp relief to Treehorn's space, which I have already described as modern in a vaguely 1950s, International-Style way, signaling not the displacement of the upper class by the haute bourgeoisie but rather their coexistence, like the residual and emergent in the current mode of production. Lebowski's house, moreover, inhabited as it is by a wheelchair-bound patriarch, provides us with another link between this film and Hawks's *The Big Sleep* through its evocation of the Sternwood mansion, just as Lebowski himself comes to parallel Sternwood.[32] Yet these affiliations are evoked only that we might appreciate crucial distinctions; for if Sternwood, coming as close as postwar America can to embodying the *ancien regime*, is immersed in a miasma of corruption and impotence (his daughters' real paternal inheritance), *The Big Lebowski*'s sleight of hand involves the substitution of wife for daughter in danger, an exchange sealed by the gestures to Kubrick's *Lolita* mentioned earlier. Lacan reminds us of the attenuation of the paternal function under modernity, to which we must respond that paternity remains an issue here, no matter how attenuated, in two important instances.[33] First the Dude waits for the Big Lebowski and examines photos on the wall:

> THE DUDE. These are, uh . . .
> BRANDT. Oh, those are Mr. Lebowski's children, so to speak.
> THE DUDE. Different mothers, huh?
> BRANDT. No.
> THE DUDE. Racially he's pretty cool?
> BRANDT. [laughs] They're not literally his children. They're the Little Lebowski Urban Achievers—inner city children of promise but without the necessary means for a—necessary means for a higher education. So Mr. Lebowski is committed to sending all of them to college.

Like Sternwood, the Big Lebowski has a fiercely independent daughter beyond his control—but unlike Sternwood he has transferred his desire for paternal control and authority onto the "Little Lebowski Urban Achievers," in effect transforming them into capital, tax write-offs for the Lebowski family businesses, fungible and manipulable. When in another twist on the principle of exchange the Dude is tricked into fathering Maude's child he proves himself able to do what the Big Lebowski can no longer. If Marlowe in *The Big Sleep* acts as a surrogate son for Sternwood, here the Dude trumps even the Big Lebowski's instrumental and cynical claims of Symbolic paternity; one shot shows him in a mirror decorated with a mock-up of a *Time* magazine cover, including the caption "Are you a Lebowski Achiever?,"[34] which is funny because the Dude is neither an achiever nor his son. In this second instance, the Dude is thought by Maude to be a perfect sperm donor precisely because of their different class positions, as well as their identical surnames. In neither example does the paternal function resolve into anything that we might gloss as normative, let alone "traditional." But these differing versions of paternity might be translated along a Lacanian axis, revealing that in the case of the Big Lebowski paternity is a Symbolic function, responsible for integrating children into various institutions and networks of knowledge, labor, language, and exchange; but he is also a self-styled Imaginary father, self-important and authoritarian. In contrast, the Dude seems to embody the Real father: he is, in Lacan's terms, the "Great Fucker" (Lacan 1992, 307) the one posited as the subject's biological father.[35]

What does it mean, then, that the Dude himself again confronts castration, and here in Maude's presence?

> MAUDE LEBOWSKI. Does the female form make you uncomfortable, Mr. Lebowski?
> THE DUDE. Uh, is that what this is a picture of?
> MAUDE LEBOWSKI. In a sense, yes. My art has been commended as being strongly vaginal which bothers some men. The word itself makes some men uncomfortable. Vagina.
> THE DUDE. Oh yeah?
> MAUDE LEBOWSKI. Yes, they don't like hearing it and find it difficult to say whereas without batting an eye a man will refer to his dick or his rod or his Johnson.
> THE DUDE. Johnson?

The repetition of "Johnson" here aligns Maude with the German nihilists who used the term earlier, condensing Maude's art with their threat of literal castration. And the mise-en-scène obliges, including a painting of scissors in the

Figure 4.4   The Dude under the sign of castration

frame with the Dude during this exchange.[36] As a painting
and especially because it is so little seen despite its pointed
affirmation of some of the themes we have been tracing,
it appears prosaic enough—indeed, it is all too legible,
too obvious in its threat of castration, and possessing little
enough of the enigmatic quality that we might wish to associate with the work of art. And yet it does bear an explicit
relation to the fetish—how could it not?—but rather than
veiling absence it renders it potentially, threateningly real.[37]
It calls for a transformation, even an undoing of particular
modes of identity and exchange, insofar as those have come
to be underwritten by the phallus. Exchange with Maude
is first undertaken on the level of dialogue, but it will later
modulate into the registers of money and sex, as she proposes he investigate her father, the Big Lebowski (although
again we never see any money change hands here) and
later as she propositions the Dude, not for pleasure but for
progeny.

> MAUDE LEBOWSKI. Do you like sex, Mr. Lebowski?
> THE DUDE. 'Scuse me?
> MAUDE LEBOWSKI. Sex. The physical act of love. Coitus. Do
>   you like it?
> THE DUDE. I was talking about my rug.
> MAUDE LEBOWSKI. You're not interested in sex?
> THE DUDE. You mean coitus?

Even if Maude's proposition follows an instrumental logic,
it is also takes a form radically different from Bunny's earlier offer. Economic exchange is cancelled, along with an
attendant objectification of the body of the woman. The rug
reappears as that contingent object that guarantees the possibility of another kind of exchange, affirming Lacan's assertion "there is no sexual relation" (Lacan 2007, 116): where
Lacan emphasizes how the phallus and fetish mediate and
structure sexual relationships, preventing access to the thing
itself, the film invests the overdetermined yet contingent
material object with desire such that it mediates exchange. As
the fetish always does, the rug eventually enables coitus here.

What the Dude's own condensations and conflations will tell us, though, has less to do with a stereotypical perception of Maude as castrating and rather more with the Dude's relative indifference to Symbolic castration as such, for if he can be unsettled by the nihilists' threat of castration in the Real, he is neither a fetishist (as we have suggested he is not), nor does he seem particularly interested in the characteristically masculine issues of mastery and narcissism that relate to the Imaginary and the ego. His confrontation with his generic double from an older historical period affirms his refusal of a phallic masculinity. The Dude finally faces the detective Da Fino (John Polito), who has also been charged with finding Bunny, and who has been spying on the Dude and Maude having sex:

> DA FINO. My name's Da Fino! I'm a private snoop! Like you, man!
> THE DUDE. Huh?
> DA FINO. A dick, man! And let me tell you something: I dig your work. Playing one side against the other—in bed with everybody—fabulous stuff, man.
> THE DUDE. I'm not a—ah, fuck it, just stay away from my fucking lady friend, man.

The Dude's truncated response is key: it performs castration in the Symbolic, cutting the dick from his utterance and thus his identity. In rejecting the designation "dick," he also refuses the mirrored identity of the hard-boiled noir detective of an older paradigm, which comes encrusted with connotations of mastery of both women and knowledge, not to mention of voyeurism and snooping. This is important particularly in this context, for not only has the Dude just helped Maude conceive but he has also, finally, solved the case, by relying not upon the unstable pair of *connaissance/méconnaissance* associated with both the mirror stage and the hard-boiled detective, but upon *savoir*: it is through his intercourse with Maude—both sexual and linguistic—that he comes to solve the case.[38] For us Da Fino's "knowledge" can only, finally, appear constraining and dominating, a reduction of lives into an utterly instrumental set of relations, as if he were a figure of the dialectic of enlightenment itself. And this representative of an older aesthetic form and an obsolete mode of knowledge comes to be discarded in favor of a mode of thought that is mimetic and intersubjective.

Unsurprisingly perhaps, the Dude's solution bears an interesting resemblance to that of Poe's famous tale. Like the letter, the woman was never purloined but in plain sight: it is not Bunny but Maude who furnishes the Dude with what he seeks, which is not only information, nor yet the fetish or the woman as body or object, but instead a realization of his own unconscious desire—the dark matter around which *savoir* must always revolve, and even in this context the cipher and enigma of that other frame, the work of art—for a little Lebowski, a child, which can now be revealed as the narrative pretext for the film's concerns with paternity as such. The Dude succeeds in having a child without being a father, since paternity in this film seems irredeemably mired in problems associated with class, power, and money, the legacies of the Symbolic and Imaginary father in this contemporary moment. He creates without dominating.

If this works at the level of the Dude's character, though, it can only seem banal in the broader frame of the film itself, offering as it does on this larger level the substitution of one generic frame—comedy and the family romance, however broadly construed or unorthodox in its configuration—for another—the noir pastiche. Maude's desire complicates Lacan's conception of feminine sexuality, since she seems to desire neither the phallus nor an absolute Other (although as we have seen the Dude seems to approach this in his class position relative to hers)—her "strongly vaginal" paintings would suggest she is situated beyond the phallus, both in terms of her art and in relation to her desire for motherhood outside of the Oedipal family.[39] However, if Maude's desires challenge these various Symbolic and patriarchal regimes, it seems barely tolerable to conceive of the Dude as possessing unconscious desires as such, let alone as being a parent, precisely because of his attenuated status, whether this attenuation is conceived of in terms of his status as a "bum" or a cliché or in terms of the film's own embrace of a particular postmodern aesthetic that cancels the category of deep character in that older, modernist sense. This returns us to the problematic with which we began. We have not yet made the dialectical turn that will get us past a need to dwell on a depth. For if this analysis has succeeded in estranging this film in order to render legible another logic—a logic that stresses the roles of exchange and fetishism in relation to identity and that challenges or complements the aleatory and provisional aspects of the narrative to suggest another set of determinants, structural, psychic and economic—it has done so at the risk of showing itself to be beholden to a *méconnaissance*, a form of knowledge that the Dude himself, for all his limits, rejects, and that puts the cultural analyst in the place of the private detective of that older, now discredited type. To conclude, then, without being a dick, we might locate in this film, as in all art, a challenge to theory, cultural analysis, and thought as such, insofar as they tend toward mastery, even insofar as they are bound, like the older philosophical aesthetics against which Adorno rages, to a kind of identity thinking, a reduction of the work to its concept. Indeed, maybe the best advice this film has for us has something to do with reconciling us to our lack, if not castration—our lack of totalizing knowledge, or better, our lack of an adequate conception of totality as such. It is precisely this knowledge that the work longs to supply, were there a context in which it could be apprehended and realized.

But we may turn the issue around, too, and argue, following Adorno's negative dialectic, that it is in the very particularities of the work of art, in those aspects that necessarily escape our efforts to slot it into a preexisting system, that its truth value is to be found. And in this respect I return to the quotation that gives this chapter its title—"Jackie Treehorn treats objects like women!"—which I would hope has modulated from its dumb phenomenal appearance to an evocation of the tangled conflations of fetishism and the commodity, sex and the social, and art and porn, to which we can now add an appropriately stupid and literal reading that is not merely the bad retelling of a joke.[40] For this is where we should ultimately locate fetishistic disavowal: in our response to the Dude's critique. We know very well that he is a burned-out old hippie, but all the same he speaks the truth—indeed, it is precisely his status as a burnout that legitimates our reading here, as we may then attend the letter of his speech in its brute exactitude. We need to read his outburst literally and not as a critique, as the Dude invites us to traverse fetishism, to see transformed our desire for commodities that seem uncannily alive and for people transformed into objects, and to see instead objects in their noumenal plenitude. It is an invitation to ask what would happen if we came to treat objects like women, if we came to grasp fully the mystified labor that went into their production, if we became true materialists. But it is also a question about the myths of history and the history of myth, as both Bunny and Maude dramatize not just how women become things for film—variously porn star, femme fatale, castrator/castrated, object of desire, and so on—but also how these limited and limiting roles can be rewritten and how these parts, subject to exchange, can instead resolve into something more like wholes. These are questions that can only be posed from the other side of fetishism, as it were—from a point where women are no longer objects and men no longer masters, from a point where critique might modulate from a denunciation of reification and alienation as given to a view of their redemptive possibilities. Not just two types of fetishism, then, but necessarily three, as art, coming from the fetish, returns to it again to offer a glimpse of a world transformed.

NOTES

INTRODUCTION

1. Exemplary for me at least is Simon Jarvis's *Adorno: A Critical Introduction* (1998).
2. The reference is, of course, to David Bordwell and Noel Carroll's *Post Theory* (Madison: U of Wisconsin Press P, 1996).

CHAPTER 1

1. But see, for a bravura reading of singularity and distinction in Adorno, Robert Hullot-Kentor "Right Listening and a New Type of Human Being," in *Things beyond Resemblance* (New York: Columbia UP, 2006), 193–209.
2. For a much richer consideration of some of these contradictions, see Robert Hullot-Kentor, "What is Mechanical Reproduction?" in *Things beyond Resemblance* (New York: Columbia UP, 2006), 136–53.
3. There are, of course, many crucial consequences for feminist thought in Adorno's link between the Sirens and nature. See, for example, Rebecca Comay, "Adorno's Siren Song," *New German Critique* 81 (2000): 21–48.
4. It is also thus for Lee Edelman (1994), in his stunning reading of *The Maltese Falcon*, "Plasticity, Paternity, Perversity: Freud's 'Falcon,' Huston's 'Freud.'" While my uses of *das ding* and later the phallus owe much to the context that Edelman provides here, I will also develop them in another direction, particularly that afforded by Lacan's reference to Kant.
5. For a reading of *das ding*'s relation to comedy and the Marx Brothers particularly, see Paul Flaig, "Lacan's Harpo," *Cinema Journal* 50(4; 2011): 98–116. Parenthetically, one must wonder why Žižek never went to town on this passage.
6. At another point in the narrative the film will seek to communicate Spade's dispossession of and from his self, though this time, crucially, through the image. Drugged by Gutman, the camera adopts a distinctively subjective perspective nowhere else in evidence in the film,

as we are treated to a blurry point-of-view shot meant to dramatize or represent Spade's consciousness dissolving (Figure 1.3). This is one of very few expressionist touches *The Maltese Falcon* gives us, unless we wish to count some of the stylized low-angle shots, too.

7. Pointedly, the *flâneur*, with his "reception in distraction" is for Robert Hullot-Kentor (2006) the very model for Benjamin's ideal cinema audience—see his "What is Mechanical Reproduction?," especially 146.

8. Although, as Google tells me, this absolute particularity can be absolutely mine, from Amazon or eBay, with prices ranging from $50 to $185 depending on whether one wishes an authentic replica or whatever the opposite of that might be.

Figure 1.3   Sam Spade drugged by Gutman

CHAPTER 2

1. See Naremore, *More than Night: Film Noir in its Contexts* (Berkley: U of California P, 2007). For a much-extended investigation of the pulps, see Paula Rabinowitz, *Black & White & Noir: America's Pulp Modernism* (New York: Columbia UP, 2002).

2. See John Sutherland's obituary of Spillane: "Mickey Spillane," *The Guardian* (July 18, 2006, http://www.guardian.co.uk/books/2006/jul/18/culture.obituaries).

3. Claude Chabrol, no less, was familiar enough with the dialectical principle here in his notes on the film: "It has chosen to create

itself out of the worst material to be found, the most deplorable, the most nauseous product of a genre in a state of putrefaction: a Mickey Spillane story" (1985, 163).

4. See Sutherland's obituary.

5. In what is surely one of the most crucial readings of this film, Caryl Flinn argues that the "excess" of the feminine voice functions as a critique of film's visual register, coded as masculine and patriarchal. My argument owes a great debt to her insights. See Flinn 1986.

6. For Fredric Jameson, noir's disembodied voices gesture toward that style's emergence out of a now-eclipsed radio culture: "Both hard-boiled detective stories and film noir are indeed structurally distinguished by the fundamental fact of the voice-over, which signals in advance the closure of the events to be narrated just as surely as it marks the operative presence of an essentially radio aesthetic which has no equivalent in the earlier novel or silent cinema" (Jameson 1993, 36).

7. Indeed, for Joan Copjec (following Pascal Bonitzer) and her analysis of Soberin, ultimately "the voice . . . dies in the body" (1994, 184). It will be my contention that the woman's voice follows another trajectory.

8. In *Seminar VIII*, his seminar on transference in the analytic situation, Lacan introduces the *agalma* as related to both the phallus and *objet petit a*. For Lacan, Alcibiades in Plato's *Symposium* demonstrates the logic of transference when he refers to Socrates as possessing the *agalma*: a treasure imagined within an indifferent vessel. See Lacan 1991, 163–78.

9. For Freud, as well as for many who have traced the image of the Medusa, the monster's head is an image of feminine genitals; and as such, "the terror of Medusa is the terror of castration that is linked to the sight of something" (1963, 23). But the Great Whatsit, as we shall see, goes rather further than this.

10. An important exception here, and one which I must force to stand in for others, is Columbo, as Žižek notes: there is never any question of Columbo accumulating and adjudicating clues and motives to produce a satisfying history and interpretation of the crime, which of necessity has occurred before the detective's entrance. Rather he always already knows the identity of the murderer, and thus each show consists of his toying with the guilty party until the murderer betrays himself or herself. See Žižek 2006a, 28.

11. There are far too many studies of noir's ambivalent representations and interrogations of masculinity to list here, but see Frank Krutnik's *In a Lonely Street: Film Noir, Genre, Masculinity* (1991).

12. While there is certainly no shortage of uncanny separations of the voice and body in noir, I must also add the example of *Laura* (1944).

As Joan Copjec points out, it is not just that the film's narrator, Waldo Lydecker, narrates it from an extradiegetic space, even from beyond the grave, but also that this space is doubly marked by technology: by Lydecker's voice on the radio and his final utterance after his death from the studio itself. See Copjec 2002,160.

13. And it is a desire that is shared: "I was out for two hours after you flipped me," Sugar later tells Hammer, despite the fact we see Sugar fall backward. This is not a continuity error; rather, we might suggest Sugar flips, abandons himself to a pleasure, a bliss, even a *jouissance* that has left him unconscious.

14. Christina's status as a Christ figure is further glossed by J. P. Telotte. See Telotte 1989, 210.

15. See Roland Barthes, "The Grain of the Voice, " in *Image Music Text*, trans. Stephen Heath (New York: Hill and Wang, 1977), 179–89.

16. More pertinent, perhaps, is Hammer's prone body, face down on the bed, offered for penetration from behind, if only from the doctor's needle—this, then, is the truth of Hammer's desire, what he cannot admit to consciousness, what must be re-membered. He will later put Evello in his former place—that is, bound face-down and spread-eagled on the bed—where the gangster is then fatally penetrated by Sugar's knife.

17. Mladen Dolar, in "If Music Be the Food of Love," writes, "Music is ascribed the power of being able to attain God's mercy and win the heart of one's beloved, and this is also the place of its ineradicable ambiguity—music is at one and the same time the epitome of transcendence and of sensuality and eroticism" (2002, 10). That is, opera also affirms the mutual implication of body and spirit by way of the voice.

18. This is Fredric Jameson's point, which he attributes to Miriam Hansen, among others: "It does not seem abusive to generalize these insights into the general hypothesis that whenever other media appear within film, their deeper function is to set off and demonstrate the latter's ontological primacy" (Jameson 1992, 84 n. 19). Significantly, for all the media and technology figured here—radio, answering machine—television is conspicuously left unthematized: it is present only in the apartment of the journalist Ray Dyker, where, tellingly, it is switched off. It remains a deferred question, in this agon between media and art, why the film's own conflict and competition with the small screen is excluded.

19. Charles Bitsch, "Surmultipliee," *Cahiers du cinéma*, 51 (October 1955): 3.

20. This is also a kiss/shot that reverses the climax of Spillane's novel, in which Hammer shoots the woman—an analyst—in the stomach.

21. See David Bordwell, *The Films of Carl-Theodor Dreyer* (Berkeley: U of California P, 1981), 66–92.

22. In a more muted vein, there seems also to be an affinity between these two directors on the level of composition and camera placement—in particular, the severe geometries of light that frame Lily/ Gabrielle as she opens the Great Whatsit seem pointedly Dreyer-esque. While not, to be sure, as utterly free as Dreyer's in multiplying and ultimately flattening three-dimensional perspectives onto the two-dimensional space of the screen, Aldrich's camera nonetheless often assumes impossible perspectives, as the many cheat shots in this film attest. Likewise, the film's obsession with staircases seems to assert something about the radical incommensurabilities of all the different spaces on offer here, particularly insofar as they, like Dreyer's more extreme experiments, challenge spatial continuity.

CHAPTER 3

1. That said, it would be worth retaining the sense in which, as Fredric Jameson writes, "an equal flourishing of grade-B forms, punk films, and conspiratorial or paranoid artifacts, whole willful choices of sleaze and imperfection, of junk and garbage landscapes, and of deliberately shoddy or garish color when not outright black-and-white stock, mark the will to inauthenticity as the sign of a now socially marginalized Real and as the only true space of authenticity in a spurious image culture dominated by a hegemonic postmodernism" (1990b, 218). I will return to this point; but for now, I take this issue of trash culture to be less expressive of a desire for authenticity—always a slippery and variable cultural concept—than indicative of the ubiquity of commodity culture.

2. See Jameson 1998, especially 82–85.

3. This is a relationship he most fully explores in his "Cultural Criticism and Society" (Adorno 1967a).

4. See Georg Lukács, Preface to *The Theory of the Novel,* trans. Anna Bostock (Cambridge, MA: MIT P, 1971), 22.

5. Stallabrass offers a provocative and critical aesthetics of trash that emphasizes its collective production, and my own gloss here owes a great deal to his tremendous essay.

6. Benjamin's references to surrealism are extensive, but see particularly, Benjamin, "Surrealism: The Last Snapshot of the European Intelligentsia," in *Selected Writings Vol. 2,* ed. M. W. Jennings, H. Eiland, and G. Smith (Cambridge, MA: Belknap P, 1999), 207–21.

7. Benjamin's philosophical interest in surrealism is certainly allied with his hashish experiments; for a very useful overview, see Marcus Boon, "Walter Benjamin and Drug Literature," in *On Hashish,* by Walter

Benjamin (Cambridge, MA: Belknap P, 2006), 1–12. For a detailed
comparison of Benjamin and Adorno on surrealism, see Richard
Wolin, "Benjamin, Adorno, Surrealism," in *The Semblance of Subjectivity*, eds. Tom Huhn and Lambert Zuidervaart (Cambridge, MA:
MIT P, 1997), 93–122.

8. His classic text here is, of course, his *History and Class Consciousness:
Studies in Marxist Dialectics*, trans. Rodney Livingstone (Cambridge,
MA: MIT P, 1971).

9. See David Rodowick, "An Elegy for Theory," *October* 122 (2007):
91–109.

10. See *The Political Unconscious: Narrative as a Socially Symbolic Act*
(Ithaca, NY: Cornell UP, 1981), 102.

11. See "Totality as Conspiracy," in Jameson 1992, 9–84.

12. Here *Repo Man* exacts revenge against the state trooper that so effectively menaced Janet Leigh in *Psycho*. And in a very-much related
sense, later in the film Otto will pour scalding coffee on the rent-
a-cop Plettschner, payback for Gloria Grahame's disfigurement in
Fritz Lang's *The Big Heat* (1953). Intertextually at least, this seems a
feminist film, if not in itself.

13. Just like Pablo Picasso, Jonathan Richmond tells us on the soundtrack.

14. See particularly Stanley Cavell's *The World Viewed: Reflections on the
Ontology of Film* (Cambridge, MA: Harvard UP, 1979) and Gilles
Deleuze's *Cinema 2: The Time Image*, trans. Hugh Tomlinson and
Robert Galeta (Minneapolis: U of Minnesota P, 1989). Rodowick
discusses the ethical frames of both in his "An Elegy for Theory,"
affirming a broadly philosophically informed ethical orientation as a
potential way forward for a moribund film theory.

15. No offence meant to Malibu drivers past or present. Indeed, this model's trashy fate is due in part to its success: it began as a "top-line" sub-
series of the Chevelle, remaining in Chevrolet's product lineup to the
present. However, its very success and its former status as a "top-line"
model both serve to account for the ubiquity of older versions on the
road, then and now: that ubiquity makes a lie of its distinctive status.

16. To be fair, Duke has, just before bursting into the store, expressed a
desire for something more than a life of crime, though this desire and
its expression cannot be affirmed as utopian in an unqualified sense:

DUKE. I've been thinking. Now that we've got some money and
Archie's gone, don't you think it's time we settle down? Get a
little house. I want you to have my baby.
DEBBIE. Why?
DUKE. Well, I don't know. Everybody does it. And it just seems
like the thing to do, and . . .
DEBBIE. Asshole.

A dream of freedom coincides with social domination, and were this marriage come to pass it seems easy enough to imagine it resembling that of Otto's parents, though with butyl nitrate replacing the pot.

CHAPTER 4

1. See especially Adorno 1997, 199–225.
2. *Das ding* also bears a fundamental relation to *jouissance*: as the forbidden object of incestuous desire—that is, the mother—it comes to structure the subject's relation to the pleasure principle as such. For Lacan the pleasure principle's very function is to keep the subject at a distance from this object, whose possession, were it possible, could only bring pain. See Lacan 1992, 43–70.
3. For his most systematic articulation of his method, see Žižek 2006b, particularly 44–47.
4. In this Žižekian sense critique is neurotic—that is, we understand objects and phenomena too quickly, a problem exacerbated by the ways in which, under postmodernism, culture and commodities seem to come to us packaged with their own interpretation.
5. And indeed it is arguable whether there is ever, finally, in Hegel anything like the triumphal synthesis and teleology often ascribed to the dialectic. For another description, and one entailing *das ding* and repetition, see Žižek 2012, especially 491–506.
6. For example, "Despite the preponderance of the object, the thingness of the world is also phenomenal. It tempts the subject to ascribe their own social circumstances of production to the noumena. This is elaborated in Marx's chapter on fetishes" (Adorno 1973, 189).
7. Reneé Heberle describes the use of Adorno's conception of myth and history in relation to feminist concerns as follows: "Where some feminists have shown the historicity of presumably natural qualities of sexed existence, others have shown the irrational, mythic, naturalizing force of historically constituted notions of masculinity and femininity" (Heberle 2006, 5).
8. Something similar seems to be at work when the Dude takes a stand in the cab from the police station:

> THE DUDE. Jesus, man, can you change the station?
> DRIVER. Fuck you man! You don't like my fucking music, get your own fucking cab!
> THE DUDE. I've had a—
> DRIVER. I pull over and kick your ass out, man!
> THE DUDE. —had a rough night, and I hate the fucking Eagles, man—
> DRIVER. That's it! Outta this fucking cab!

At first the stakes seem notably lower—aesthetic judgment compared to taking a stand on pornography. Indeed, given what we know of the Dude, we might expect him to like "Peaceful Easy Feeling." But this is precisely the point: the Dude will not be identified with what he knows to be commodity music, which cannot for him function to assert or reveal his interiority or essence; and he, along with the film itself, will come to reject the value of music in terms of its exchange value—how it might have in this context of a narrative hero linked to the 1960s devolved into an exercise in pandering nostalgia. In short, music will be deployed in the film pointedly to frustrate identification and exchange, in a manner fully consonant with other paths we will go on to trace. For a fuller consideration of the role of popular music in the film see Diane Pecknold 2009.

9. See for example Jean Baudrillard, *Symbolic Exchange and Death*, trans. Iain Hamilton Grant (London: Sage, 1993).

10. I borrow this idea of an "end" of fetishism from Jean-Michel Rabaté, who in turn has taken it from Breton and Aragon's conception of hysteria in the *Surrealist Manifesto*. For Rabaté, the surrealists' "end of hysteria" evinces pertinent parallels with the putative "end of theory." See Rabaté 2002, 10–11, and André Breton, "Manifeste du Surréalisme," in *Oeuvres Complètes I*, eds. M. Bonnet, P. Bernier, E-A. Hubert and J. Pierre (Paris: Gallimard, Pléiade, 1988), 326.

11. Paradoxically, this de-differentiation between the two fetishisms also has the effect of problematizing the gender-specific histories of each, under which sexual fetishism is for Freud masculine, while commodity fetishism typically evokes a feminine or at least feminized consumer. See Freud "Fetishism" in *The Standard Edition of the Complete Psychological Works of Sigmund Freud, Vol. XXI*, ed. James Strachey (London: Hogarth, 1961), 150.

12. As Jameson writes, "it would be comical to wish the social burden of bourgeois respectability and elaborate moral taboo back into existence merely to re-endow the sex drive with the value of a political act" (1992, 12).

13. But on this point see Whitebook 2004.

14. In a sentence of truly epic and very Adornoian density, Fredric Jameson follows this logic further:

> Speculation on the consequences of just such a general removal of the need for a survival instinct leads us well beyond the bounds of Adorno's social life-world and class style (and our own), and into a Utopia of misfits and oddballs, in which the constraints for uniformization and conformity have been removed, and human beings grow wild like plants in a state of nature: not the beings of Thomas More, in whom sociality has

been implanted by way of the miracle, of the utopian text, but rather those of the opening of Altman's *Popeye*, who, no longer fettered by the constraints of a now oppressive sociality, blossom into the neurotics, compulsives, obsessives, paranoids, and schizophrenics whom our society considers sick but who, in a world of true freedom, may make up the flora and fauna of "human nature" itself. (1990a, 102)

While I might wish to stop short of including paranoids and schizophrenics as figures of subjective freedom (as does the Deleuze of *Anti-Oedipus*, for that matter)—such an inclusion would have to ask after the fate of pain under utopia in a way that resisted aestheticizing what is experienced as suffering—nonetheless *The Big Lebowski's* panoply of characters, from the grotesque to the merely eccentric, tends to confirm Jameson's point. Though it cannot be that the principle of self-preservation is absent in the film's world, at least in the case of the Dude—and particularly in his characteristic abiding—we get a fitful intimation of what such freedom may be like.

15. Famously, Howard Hawks and star Humphrey Bogart got into an argument over whether the Sternwood's chauffeur was murdered or committed suicide. They sent a wire to author Raymond Chandler asking him to settle the issue, but the author was at a loss, too. In both films, then, narrative causality as such seems hardly to be an issue—although for very different reasons.

16. Analogous to the seeming impossibility of economic exchange is the film's representation of verbal exchange in terms of non sequiturs. Perhaps one example can come stand for all the others. Here the Dude is at the bowling alley, outlining his theory that Bunny has kidnapped herself:

   THE DUDE. It's all a goddamn fake. Like Lenin said, look for the person who will benefit. And you will, uh, you know, you'll, uh, you know what I'm trying to say—
   DONNY. I am the Walrus.

17. It is of course Laura Mulvey's "Visual Pleasure and Narrative Cinema" (2004) that paradigmatically explores the relationship of the filmic gaze to voyeurism and fetishism.

18. Fritz Lang's *Scarlet Street* (1945) is relevant here, too. Kitty, the femme fatale who has been encouraging the advances of the repressed amateur painter Chris Cross, offers him her toenails: "Paint me Chris! I'm sure it'll be a masterpiece!" Her invitation in that context suggests the extent to which Kitty, if not Chris, understands the relations of fetishism and sublimation to art, especially in terms of art's marketing and economic value.

19. Of course, when the Dude is discussing the possible loss of his Johnson to the nihilists, Donny (Steve Buscemi) pointedly asks, "What do you need that for Dude?" What indeed—as we will consider later, the film suggests that his Johnson is necessary for its use, rather than for its potential or Symbolic exchange.

20. It should be noted that this choice differs significantly from Žižek's favorite: "Your money or your life!" The Dude's dilemma has aspects of this "forced choice," too, since in both instances he must submit to castration—the difference here is to be located in the distinction between castration in the Symbolic and in the Real.

21. See, for example, *Babes in Arms* (1939).

22. Of course, as a fantasy/spectacle, this sequence itself accords with the logic that Mulvey details: it arrests or punctuates the narrative, which is, of course, concerned with ascertaining guilt, even if finally it does not succeed in doing so.

23. See Chapter 2, note 18.

24. This is Jameson's point:

> The irony and impertinence of the Kant reference (the Culture Industry has developed a streamlined form of Kantian schematism for its products [*Dialectic of Enlightenment* 127–28, ref. modified] draws its density from the privileged position of aesthetics in the period of classical German idealism, and at the beginnings of capitalism: a position based not on some canon of masterpieces but rather on the space still offered for the exercise of a non-alienated subjectivity that was neither business or science, neither morality nor pure reason. This enclave is what the Culture Industry now begins to colonize, a kind of last frontier and final unexplored territory for the dialectic of Enlightenment. (1990a, 107–8)

25. Like a 1964 Chevy Malibu with aliens in the trunk!

26. See Herbert Marcuse, *One-Dimensional Man* (Boston: Beacon, 1991), 56–83; and Slavoj Žižek, *The Sublime Object of Ideology* (London: Verso, 1989), 11–54.

27. I take this also to be Judith Roof's point in "Size Matters" (2009), although for her the film's privileged images for the breakdown of masculinist economies are its fluids.

28. See especially Adorno and Horkheimer 2002, 1–34.

29. See especially William Pietz, "The Problem of the Fetish 1" *Res* 9 (1985): 5–17; "The Problem of the Fetish 2" *Res* 13 (1987): 23–45; "The Problem of the Fetish 3" *Res* 16 (1988): 105–23; and Homi Bhabha, *The Location of Culture* (London: Routledge, 1994).

30. "Not the compromised second draft," the Dude specifies.

31. We might here also return to the figure of Marty, the Dude's landlord, whose cycle or quintet we have already discussed in terms of modern dance. But it might be possible to wonder if his art bears some distant affiliation to the happenings and performances of the 1960s, modes that seem relevant for their implicit rejection of the art-object's commodification, as well as of its object status as such. What would then be his "retreat" back into dance echoes in an aesthetic register the Dude's own retreat from radical politics.

32. While we have already remarked the important formal likenesses that bind *The Big Lebowski* and *The Big Sleep*, we should note the substantial differences that distinguish Bogart's Marlowe and Bridges's the Dude, the former as a version of the subject-supposed-to-know, imposing a retroactive sense of order on chaotic and seemingly random events, while the latter seems largely to be purely reactive, responding to the violent intensities of this world. This distance between the two figures might suggest something important about that historical passage from modernity to postmodernity, from analysis and causality to a flux of ahistorical intensities.

33. See, for example, Lacan (2007), 117–23.

34. Neither is this even a minimal mirror stage for the Dude, since the caption emphasizes the profound gulf between him and this specific Imaginary. For Lacan, identification with the image is of course a kind of misrecognition, but it would be better in this context to refer to the French *méconnaissance*. Lacan distinguishes between *connaissance/méconnaissance*, which are delusory in their implications of mastery, integrity, and completion, and *savoir*, which is necessarily incomplete and intersubjective, part of the Symbolic rather than the Imaginary register. See "The Subversion of the Subject and the Dialectic of Desire in the Freudian Unconscious," in Lacan (2006), 671–702. I will return to this distinction.

35. The Dude would seem to agree:

THE BIG LEBOWSKI. What makes a man, Mr. Lebowski?

. . .

THE DUDE. I don't know, sir.

THE BIG LEBOWSKI. Is it . . . is it being prepared to do the right thing? Whatever the price? Isn't that what makes a man?

THE DUDE. Sure. That and a pair of testicles.

36. This intersection of Maude and the nihilists will be condensed in another of the Dude's dreams, in which he finds himself pursued by the nihilists, each dressed as the tailor from Hoffman's *Struwwelpeter*, wielding scissors.

37. Certainly Maude's work replies to a tradition whose essence might be found in Renoir's claim "I paint with my prick." Rather than

insisting upon identity, presence, and value as guaranteed by a pro-
miscuous and elusive signifier, can we say that Maude's art seeks to
give body to absence itself? Only if what might have been fetishisti-
cally labeled an absence comes to be seen as a positive presence—that
is, "strongly vaginal"—in its own right.

38. For Lacan, the distinction between *connaissance* and *savoir* registers
the difference between Imaginary and Symbolic knowledge: as his
description of the mirror stage suggests, Imaginary *connaissance* is
always *méconnaissance*, a misrecognition of the image as oneself,
which contributes to the ego's fantasy of integrity and mastery. *Savoir*
is the goal of analysis, entailing both a knowledge of the subject's
place in the Symbolic order as well as a realization of the truth of
one's unconscious desire—as Dylan Evans emphasizes, "Symbolic
knowledge does not reside in any particular subject, nor in the Other
(which is not a subject but a locus), but is intersubjective" (Evans
1996, 94). See Lacan 2006, 75–81. On *savoir*, see Jacques Lacan,
"Knowledge, a Means of *jouissance*," in *The Other Side of Psychoanalysis*, trans. Russell Grigg (New York: Norton, 2007), 39–53.
Ironically, when the Dude tries to behave as a traditional detective
he comes face to face with that signifier of power and integrity:
during his interview with the Dude, Treehorn takes a phone call,
scribbles on a writing pad, and then excuses himself, taking the sheet
of paper. The Dude then takes advantage of his absence to discover
what was written on the pad by the phone by using a pencil to reveal
the impressions left. Jackie Treehorn's mystic writing pad reveals a
homunculus with a ponderous erection, mocking the Dude's—and
the detective's—pretensions to knowledge.

39. See Lacan 1998.

40. For both the challenge to thought and the structural role that stupidity plays in thought, see Avital Ronell's *Stupidity* (Urbana: U of
Illinois P, 2002).

REFERENCES

Adorno, Theodor W. 1967a. "Cultural Criticism and Society." In *Prisms*. 17–34. Trans. Samuel and Shierry Weber. London: Neville Spearman.
———. 1967b. "Notes on Kafka." In *Prisms*. 243–71. Trans. Samuel and Shierry Weber. London: Neville Spearman.
———. 1967c. "A Portrait of Walter Benjamin." In *Prisms*. 227–42. Trans. Samuel and Shierry Weber. London: Neville Spearman.
———. 1967d. "Sociology and Psychology Part I." *New Left Review* 1(46): 67–80.
———. 1973. *Negative Dialectics*. Trans. E. B. Ashton. New York: Continuum.
———. 1974. *Minima Moralia: Reflections from Damaged Life*. Trans. E. F. N. Jephcott. London: Verso.
———. 1991a. "The Essay as Form." In *Notes to Literature*. Vol. 1. Trans. Shierry Weber Nicholsen, 3–23. 2 vols. New York: Columbia UP.
———. 1991b. "Trying to Understand *Endgame*." In *Notes to Literature*. Vol. 1. 241–75.
———. 1993. *Hegel: Three Studies*. Trans. Shierry Weber Nicholsen. Cambridge, MA: MIT P.
———. 1997. *Aesthetic Theory*. Trans. and ed. Robert Hullot-Kentor. Minneapolis: U of Minnesota P.
———. 1998. "Subject and Object." In *Critical Models*. Trans. Henry W. Pickford, 245–58. New York: Columbia UP.
———. 2001. *Kant's Critique of Pure Reason*. Trans. Rodney Livingstone. Ed. Rolf Tiedemann. Stanford, CA: Stanford UP.
———. 2003. "Art and the Arts." In *Can One Live After Auschwitz?* Ed. Rolf Tiedemann, 368–90. Stanford, CA: Stanford UP.
Adorno, Theodor W., and Walter Benjamin. 1999. In *The Complete Correspondence, 1928–1940*. Trans. Nicholas Walker. Ed. Henri Lonitz. Cambridge, MA: Harvard UP.
Adorno, Theodor W., and Hans Eisler. 2007. *Composing for the Films*. New York: Continuum.
Adorno, Theodor, and Max Horkheimer. 2002. *Dialectic of Enlightenment: Philosophical Fragments*. Ed. Gunzelin Schmid Noerr. Trans. Edmund Jephcott. Stanford, CA: Stanford UP.
Bazin, André. 1967. "The Ontology of the Photographic Image." In *What is Cinema?* Trans. Hugh Gray, 9–16. Berkley: U of California P.
Benjamin, Walter. 1968. "Theses on the Philosophy of History." In *Illuminations*. Trans. Harry Zohn, 253–64. New York: Schocken.

———. 1977. *The Origin of German Tragic Drama.* Trans. John Osborne. London: Verso.

———. 1999. *The Arcades Project.* Ed. Rolf Tiedemann. Trans. Howard Eiland and Kevin McLaughlin. Cambridge, MA: Belknap P.

———. 2002. "The Work of Art in the Age of Its Technological Reproducibility." In *Selected Writings, Vol. 3, 1935–1938.* 4 vols. Ed. Michael Jennings, Howard Eiland, and Gary Smith, 101–33. Cambridge, MA: Belknap P.

Bewes, Timothy. 2002. *Reification, or The Anxiety of Late Capitalism.* New York: Verso.

The Big Lebowski. Dir. Ethan Coen. 1998. Los Angeles, CA: Universal, 2011. Blu-ray.

Bordwell, David, and Noel Carroll, eds. 1996. *Post Theory.* Madison: U of Wisconsin P.

Chabrol, Claude. 1985. "Evolution of the Thriller." In *Cahiers du Cinéma: The 1950s: Neo-Realism, Hollywood, New Wave.* Ed. Jim Hillier, 158–64. Cambridge, MA: Harvard UP.

Chion, Michel. 1994. *Audio-Vision: Sound on Screen.* Trans. Claudia Gorbman. New York: Columbia UP.

Copjec, Joan. 1994. *Read My Desire: Lacan against the Historicists.* Cambridge, MA: MIT P.

———. 2002. *Imagine There's No Woman: Ethics and Sublimation.* Cambridge, MA: MIT P.

Dolar, Mladen. 2002. "If Music Be the Food of Love." In *Opera's Second Death,* Eds. Slavoj Žižek and Mladen Dolar. 1–102. New York: Routledge.

———. 2006. *A Voice and Nothing More.* Cambridge, MA: MIT P.

Edelman, Lee. 1994. "'Plasticity, Paternity, Perversity: Freud's 'Falcon,' Huston's 'Freud.'" *American Imago* 51(1): 69–104.

Evans, Dylan. 1996. *An Introductory Dictionary of Lacanian Psychoanalysis.* London: Routledge.

Flinn, Caryl. 1986. "Sound, Woman and the Bomb: Dismembering the 'Great Whatsit' in *Kiss Me Deadly.*" *Wide Angle* 8(3–4): 115–27.

Freud, Sigmund. 1963. "Medusa's Head." In *Sexuality and the Psychology of Love.* Ed. P. Rieff, 212–13. New York: Collier.

———. 1974. "On Narcissism: An Introduction." In *The Standard Edition of the Complete Psychological Works of Sigmund Freud.* Vol. 14. Ed. and trans. James Strachey, in collaboration with Anna Freud, assisted by Alex Strachey and Alan Tyson, 67–102. London: The Hogarth Press and the Institute of Psycho-Analysis, 1957.

Hansen, Miriam. 2012. *Cinema and Experience: Siegfried Kracauer, Walter Benjamin, and Theodor W. Adorno.* Berkley: U of California P.

Heberle, Reneé. 2006. "Introduction." In *Feminist Interpretations of Theodor Adorno*. Ed. Reneé Heberle, 1-20. University Park: Pennsylvania State UP.

Hegel, G. W. F. 1977. *The Phenomenology of Spirit*. Trans. A. V. Miller. Oxford, Eng.: Oxford UP.

Helming, Steven. 2005. "'Immanent Critique' and 'Dialectical Mimesis' in Adorno and Horkheimer's *Dialectic of Enlightenment*." *boundary 2* 32(3): 97–117.

Hullot-Kentor, Robert. 2006. *Things beyond Resemblance: Collected Essays on Theodor W. Adorno*. New York: Columbia UP.

———. 2011. "What Barbarism Is?" *The Brooklyn Rail*. June 8, 2011. http://brooklynrail.org/2010/02/art/what-barbarism-is.

Jameson, Fredric. 1988. "Imaginary and Symbolic in Lacan." *The Ideologies of Theory: Essays 1971–1986*, 75–115. Vol. 1. 2 vols. Minneapolis: U of Minnesota P.

———. 1990a. *Late Marxism*. London: Verso.

———. 1990b. *Signatures of the Visible*. New York: Routledge.

———. 1991. *Postmodernism, or, The Cultural Logic of Late Capitalism*. Durham, NC: Duke UP.

———. 1992. *The Geopolitical Aesthetic: Cinema and Space in the World System*. Bloomington: Indiana UP.

———. 1993. "The Synoptic Chandler." In *Shades of Noir*. Ed. Joan Copjec, 33–56. New York: Verso.

———. 1998. *The Cultural Turn*. New York: Verso.

———. 2002. *A Singular Modernity*. London: Verso.

———. 2005. "Utopia and Its Antinomics." *Archaeologies of the Future: The Desire Called Utopia and Other Science Fictions*, 142–69. London: Verso.

Jarvis, Simon. 1998. *Adorno: A Critical Introduction*. New York: Routledge.

Jennemann, David. 2007. *Adorno in America*. Minneapolis: U of Minnesota P.

Kiss Me Deadly. Dir. Robert Aldrich. 1955. New York: Criterion Collection, 2011. Blu-ray.

Klinger, Barbara. 2010. "Becoming Cult: *The Big Lebowski*, Replay Culture and Male Fans." *Screen* 51(1):1–20.

Krutnik, Frank. 1991. *In a Lonely Street: Film Noir, Genre, Masculinity*. London: Routledge.

Lacan, Jacques. 1988. *The Seminar of Jacques Lacan. Book II: The Ego in Freud's Theory and in the Technique of Psychoanalysis, 1954–1955*. Ed. Jacques-Alain Miller. Trans. Sylvana Tomaselli. New York: Norton.

———. 1991. *Le Séminaire. Livre VIII. Le transfert, 1960–61*. Ed. Jacques-Alain Miller. Paris: Seuil.

———. 1992. *The Ethics of Psychoanalysis, 1959–1960*. Trans. Dennis Porter. New York: Norton.

———. 1994. *Le Séminaire. Livre IV. La relation d'objet, 1956–57*. Ed. Jacques-Alain Miller. Paris: Seuil.

———. 1998. *On Feminine Sexuality: The Limits Of Love and Knowledge, 1972–1973*. Trans. Bruce Fink. New York: Norton.

———. 2006. *Écrits: The First Complete Edition in English*. Trans. Bruce Fink in collaboration with Héloise Fink and Russell Grigg. New York: Norton.

———. 2007. *The Other Side of Psychoanalysis, 1969–1970*. Trans. Russell Grigg. New York: Norton.

The Maltese Falcon. Dir. John Huston. 1941. Burbank, CA: Warner Home Video, 2010. Blu-ray.

Marx, Karl. 1976. *Capital: A Critique of Political Economy*. Trans. Ben Fowkes. Vol. 1. Harmondsworth, Eng.: Penguin.

Marx, Karl, and Friedrich Engels. 1982. *The Communist Manifesto*. Harmondsworth, Eng.: Penguin.

———. 1978. *The Grundrisse. The Marx-Engels Reader*. 2nd ed. Ed. Robert C. Tucker, 221–93. New York: Norton.

Moretti, Franco. 2000. *The Way of the World: The Bildungsroman in European Culture*. 2nd ed. New York: Verso.

Mulvey, Laura. 2004. "Visual Pleasure and Narrative Cinema." In *Film Theory and Criticism: Introductory Readings*. 6th ed. Ed. Leo Braudy and Marshall Cohen, 837–48. New York: Oxford UP.

Nancy, Jean-Luc. 2008a. *Corpus*. New York: Fordham UP, 2008.

———. 2008b. "Icon of Fury: Claire Denis's *Trouble Every Day*." *Film-Philosophy* 12(1): 1–9.

Naremore, James. 2007. *More than Night: Film Noir in its Contexts*. Berkley: U of California P.

Pecknold, Diane. 2009. "Holding Out Hope for the Creedence: Music and the Search for the Real Thing in *The Big Lebowski*." In *The Year's Work in Lebowski Studies*. Eds. Edward P. Comentale and Aaron Jaffe, 276–94. Bloomington: Indiana UP.

Rabaté, Jean-Michel. 2002. *The Future of Theory*. Oxford: Blackwell.

Repo Man. Dir. Alex Cox. 1984. London: Eureka Entertainment, 2012. Blu-ray.

Roof, Judith. 2009. "Size Matters." In *The Year's Work in Lebowski Studies*. Eds. Edward P. Comentale and Aaron Jaffe, 410–26. Bloomington: Indiana UP.

Silver, Alain. 1996. "*Kiss Me Deadly*: Evidence of a Style." In *Film Noir Reader*. Eds. Alain Silver and James Ursini, 209–35. New York: Limelight Editions.

Silverman, Kaja. 1988. *The Acoustic Mirror: The Female Voice in Psychoanalysis and Cinema.* Bloomington: Indiana UP.

Stallabrass, Julian. 1996. "Trash." In *Gargantua: Manufactured Mass Culture*, 171–88. London: Verso.

Sutherland, John. 2006. "Mickey Spillane." *The Guardian*, July 18, 2006. http://www.guardian.co.uk/books/2006/jul/18/culture.obituaries.

Telotte, J. P. 1989. *Voices in the Dark: The Narrative Patterns of Film Noir.* Urbana-Champaign: U of Illinois P.

Whitebook, Joel. 2004. "Weighty Objects: On Adorno's Kant-Freud Interpretation." In *The Cambridge Companion to Adorno.* Ed. Tom Huhn, 51–78. Cambridge, MA: Cambridge UP.

Younger, Prakash. 2003. "Rereading Bazin's Ontological Argument." *Offscreen.* 7(7): n.p.

Žižek, Slavoj. 1996. *The Indivisible Remainder.* London: Verso.

———. 2001. *On Belief.* London: Routledge.

———. 2006a. *How to Read Lacan.* London: Granta.

———. 2006b. *The Parallax View.* Cambridge, MA: MIT P.

———. 2012. *Less than Nothing: Hegel and the Shadow of Dialectical Materialism.* London: Verso.

INDEX

CPSIA information can be obtained
at www.ICGtesting.com
Printed in the USA
LVHW051630080919
630319LV00005B/261/P